CELTIC
INVOCATIONS

CELTIC

INVOCATIONS

Selections from Volume I
of Carmina Gadelica by

ALEXANDER CARMICHAEL

Vineyard Books

TO THE FAMILY, FRIENDS, SCHOLARS
AND PUBLISHERS WHO HAVE WORKED
FOR SO MANY YEARS TO COMPLETE
AND PUBLISH THE LIFE WORK OF
ALEXANDER   CARMICHAEL

THE Gaelic decorations and initials in this edition came from Volume I of *Carmina Gadelica*. We have chosen to use the initials as decoration rather than incorporating them into the text. In all cases where they appear beside an invocation, they represent the first letter used in the Gaelic version.

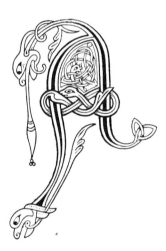

PREFACE TO
CELTIC INVOCATIONS

BEYOND a small circle of Celtic Scholars, the name of Alexander Carmichael is almost unknown. Yet there is a stamp of greatness about his work. It is both the greatness of a man and the greatness of the vanishing culture he recorded and both deserve wider recognition.

Carmichael was born in Scotland in 1832 on the island of Lismore in the Hebrides. He was educated at the University of Edinburgh and earned his living as a civil servant. "His official life was spent in Greenock, Dublin, Islay, Cornwall, Skye, Uist, Oban, Uist again, and lastly, for the sake of his childrens' education, in Edinburgh."[1]

From boyhood his true vocation was the recording of Gaelic songs, prayers, incantations, tales and customs that were preserved in the oral tradition throughout the Highlands and Islands of Scotland. "It was in Uist that he reached his full development, and got to know, as few have, the inner life of the people. His visits to Uist and the Isles continued long after his retirement and it is on record that in his 77th year he went on a collecting pilgrimage through the Northern Counties which would have tested the strength of a man in his prime."[2]

Carmichael not only recorded what he heard, but also translated it from Gaelic into English. Translations are a matter of faithfulness to the spirit as well as the letter, and in the words of Adam Bittleston, his work shows "him as one of the translators through whom a masterpiece can be reborn in a new language."[3]

[1]The words of his step-grandson, William Watson of Bangor, who has kindly helped us with the biographical details.
[2]Ibid.
[3]*The Sun Dances*, Christian Community Press, London and Edinburgh.

PREFACE

The Gaelic material that Alexander Carmichael collected stems from ancient Celtic roots. There is a great interest in the Celts today and in the allied subjects of Druids, Arthurian legends, and the great standing stones which were already ancient in Celtic times. Our particular interest is in Celtic Christianity. When Celts and Christians met, a culture, a theology and a spirituality were born that are both centrally Christian and uniquely Celtic. Celtic Christianity speaks to our own hearts and needs today, for perhaps no other Christian spirituality has shown such a deep yet simple sense of God's presence in the world. The Celtic Christians seldom left the spiritual behind in the living of their lives, nor the world behind in their prayers.

The religion, mythology, songs, and laws of the pre-Christian Celts were handed down through the years in the oral tradition. There was nothing casual about this. In Ireland, where Celtic culture flourished beyond the control of the Roman Empire, great schools taught Druids, Bards and Brehons by the oral method, and the highest degree offered took eleven years or more to attain.

Much of this material was lost—but not all. The custom of learning by heart remained and the early missionaries were unusually tolerant. Old customs and words were often "sained", that is, they were blessed with the sign of the cross and taken over into Christian practice. In consequence, many centuries later, we are able to discern in the invocations collected by Alexander Carmichael, threads of pre-Christian beliefs woven comfortably into the cloth of a living Christian faith.

AVERY BROOKE

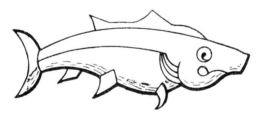

USEFUL NOTES FOR
THE READER

THE Celts had a delightful but confusing way of shifting from past to present and interlacing a variety of titles, proper names, attributes and activities. A good example may be found on p. 47. Here, in a loving chant about a cow, we suddenly realize that the word *Herdsman* is capitalized and probably refers to Christ. This is fortunate, for when it refers to the missing Herdsman being found in "the Temple", the reader has at least a chance of remembering the Biblical story of the young Jesus being sought by His parents and found "in the Temple". But then, in the very next line, one is reminded of pre-Christian Celts by invocations to "The King of the Moon" and "The King of the Sun". Of course all Christians think of God as King of sun, moon and all creation but we don't usually mix and match in the same, assured comfortable and unexplained fashion. In other prayers Christ is referred to as Chief of Chiefs. In this case the practice arose because the Celtic culture was a tribal one with many Kings or Chiefs and Christ naturally came to be thought of as the Chief above all other Chiefs.

Three Saints are often invoked: St. Patrick, St. Columba and St. Bride. Patrick and Columba are easy to explain as Patrick was the major figure in the Christianization of Ireland and Columba, who was Irish, was the major figure in the Christianization of Scotland. Columba's base for his missionary work was a monastery he founded on the Island of Iona in the Hebrides. St. Bride presents a much more complex figure.

Women were held in unusually high esteem among the Celts so it is not too surprising that St. Bridget (as Bride was known in her native Ireland) was able to found a double monastery in Kildaire (one for nuns and one for monks) of which she was the head. Enough is known of St.

9

Bride to realize that she was strong, influential and compassionate, but any truths about her as a person have become lost in other symbolic meanings. Her name was the same as that of a Celtic deity considered the patron of poetry and the useful arts. Among Christian Celts she also became the patron of aidwomen (midwives) and closely associated with the Virgin Mary. Time often slips into eternity with the Celts and in the middle of a prayer we find dates disregarded and there is Bride aiding Mary at the birth of Jesus. She is also spoken of as His Foster Mother. Fostering was very important to the Celts as they had a custom of sending their children to other families to be fostered by them for at least part of their childhood and youth. In a prayer touching on any of these subjects the name of Bride was apt to be invoked, but that far from marks the limits of the times the Celts asked her help or blessing or spoke of her with love.

The pre-Christian Celts had a great range of deities. Into their place in the hearts of the people there came not only saints but angels. Gabriel and Michael appear in both the Old and New testaments. It was Gabriel who told Mary she was to give birth to Jesus, and the archangel Michael is best known for fighting "that dragon, Satan". Celtic Christians, as is amply shown in *Celtic Invocations*, believed in a larger array of guardian angels. They often invoked three others: Uriel, Ariel and Raphael. Uriel, according to Jewish apocryphal writings, was one of the four chief archangels. Ariel is a *word* in the Bible but is usually believed to refer to Jerusalem or "altar hearth" or there is just a note saying: "meaning unknown". Apocryphal writings make it seem as if Raphael was considered to be one of the seven angels mentioned in *Revelation*. It is helpful for the reader to remember that exactly which books were to be included in the Bible was not easily settled by the early Church. Many writings were considered at least holy—if not Biblical—and were in frequent use. Even today some Christians recognize a group of Jewish apocryphal books as Scriptural and others do not.

In the hearts of the Celts it was St. Michael who held the foremost position. Not only was he the patron of the sea—which played such a large part in their lives—but to quote Alexander Carmichael, "The duty of conveying the souls of the good to the abode of bliss is assigned to

10

Michael. When the soul has parted from the body and is being weighed, the archangel of heaven and the archangel of hell preside at the beam . . . Michael and all the archangels and angels of heaven sing songs of joy when the good in the soul outweighs the bad, while the devil howls as he retreats."

To understand the spirit of Celtic Christianity probably the meaning of the word "sain" is the most useful of all. "To sain" means "to bless" or "to make the sign of the cross". The word is used often in Celtic prayers but I am thinking of it now in a larger sense to describe what happened when Christian met Celt. Christians often wince at stories of missionaries forcing Western ways on peoples of other cultures; here we may, for a moment, be proud. St. Patrick, St. Columba and their followers preached the Gospel and blessed what they found with the sign of the cross. Christ was the Chief of Chiefs, but old tales, songs, runes and customs, along with the crops, the fish, daily work and nightly sleep were sained. As also the fairies, the banshees, and the people.

A. B.

11

CONTENTS

CONTENTS

CONTENTS

THE LAND AND THE PEOPLE

THIS work consists of old lore collected during the last forty-four years. It forms a small part of a large mass of oral literature written down from the recital of men and women throughout the Highlands and Islands of Scotland, from Arran to Caithness, from Perth to St Kilda.

The greater portion of the collection has been made in the Western Isles, variously called the Outer Hebrides, the Outer Isles and the Long Island.

The Long Island is composed of a series of islands, separately known as Barra, South Uist, Benbecula, North Uist, and Harris and Lewis. This chain is one hundred and nineteen miles in length, varying from a few yards to twenty-five miles in width. Viewed from the summit of its highest link, the Long Island chain resembles a huge artificial kite stretched along the green Atlantic Ocean, Lewis forming the body, the disjointed tail trending away in the blue haze and terminating in Bearnarey of Barra.

This long series of islands is evidently the backbone of a large island, perhaps of a great continent, that extended westward beyond the Isle of the Nuns, beyond the Isle of the Monks, beyond the Isle of St Flann, beyond the Isle of St Kilda, beyond the Isle of Rockal, probably beyond the storied Isle of Rocabarraidh, and possibly beyond the historic Isle of Atlantis.

This backbone is now disarticulated like the vertebrae of some huge fossil fish, each section having a life of its own. These joints are separated by rills and channels varrying from a few feet to eight miles in width.

The Atlantic rushes through these straits and narrows into the Minch, and the Minch rushes through the straits and narrows into the

17

Atlantic, four times every twenty-four hours. The constant rushing to and fro of these mighty waters is very striking.

Many of the countless islands comprising the Outer Hebrides are indented with arms of the sea studded with rocks and islands dividing and ramifying into endless mazes, giving in some cases a coast-line of over four hundred miles within their one-mile entrance. No mind could conceive, no imagination could realise, the disorderly distribution of land and water that is to be seen in those Outer Islands, where mountain and moor, sand and peat, rock and morass, reef and shoal, fresh-water lake and salt-water loch, in wildest confusion strive for mastery.

The formation of the Long Island is Laurentian gneiss, with some outcrops of Cambrian at Aoi, Lewis, and four examples of trap at Lochmaddy, Uist. The rocks everywhere show ice action, being smoothed and polished, grooved and striated from hill to sea—the grooves and striae lying east and west or thereby.

There are no trees in the Long Island except some at Rodail, Harris, and a few at Stornoway, Lewis. The wind and spray of the Atlantic are inimical to trees under present climatic conditions. There are evidences, however, that there were trees in historic and prehistoric times.

It is said that a prince of Lewis forsook a Norse princess and married a native girl. The princess vowed by Odin, Thor, and Frea, and by all the other gods and goddesses of her fathers, to avenge the insult, and she sent her witch to burn the woods of Lewis. The tradition of the burning of these woods is countenanced by the presence of charred trees in peat-moss in many places. It is on record that a Norse prince married a native Barra girl, but whether or not this was the prince of Lewis is uncertain.

There are many evidences that the sea has gained upon the land in the Long Island. In the shore and in the sea, peat-moss, tree-roots, sessile reeds, stone dykes, dwellings and temples may be seen, while pieces of moss, trees and masonry have been brought up from time to time by hooks and anchors in from ten to twenty fathoms of water.

Immense stretches of sandy plains run along the Atlantic border of the Outer Hebrides. These long reaches of sessile sand are locally called machirs—plains. They are singularly bleak, barren, and shelterless in winter. In summer, however, these 'machairs' are green and grassy, comforting to the foot, pleasing to the eye, and deliciously fragrant, being covered with strongly aromatic plants and flowers.

But the charm of these islands lies in their people—goodly to see, brave to endure, and pleasing to know.

The population of the Long Island is about fourty-four thousand. Of these, about fourty-four familes occupy two-thirds of the whole land, the crofters, cottars, and the poor who exist upon the poor, being confined to the remaining third. These are crowded upon one another like sheep in a pen.

There are no intermediate farms, no gradation holdings, to which the industrious crofter might aspire, and become a benefit to himself, an example to his neighbour, and a lever to his country.

The people of the Outer Isles, like the people of the Highlands and Islands generally, are simple and law-abiding, common crime being rare and serious crime unknown among them. They are good to the poor, kind to the stranger, and courteous to all. During all the years that I lived and travelled among them, night and day, I never met with incivility, never with rudeness, never with vulgarity, never with aught but courtesy. I never entered a house without the inmates offering me food or apologising for their want of it. I never was asked for charity in the West, a striking contrast to my experience in England, where I was frequently asked for food, for drink, for money, and that by persons whose incomes would have been wealth to the poor men and women of the West. After long experience of his tenants, the late Mr John Gordon said:—'The Uist people are born gentlemen—Nature's noblemen.'

Gaelic oral literature was widely diffused, greatly abundant, and excellent in quality—in the opinion of scholars, unsurpassed by anything similar in the ancient classics of Greece or Rome.

Many causes contributed towards these attainments—the crofting system, the social customs, and the evening 'ceilidh.' In a crofting community the people work in unison in the field during the day, and discuss together in the house at night. This meeting is called 'ceilidh'—a word that throbs the heart of the Highlander wherever he be. The 'ceilidh' is a literary entertainment where stories and tales, poems and ballads, are rehearsed and recited, and songs are sung, conundrums are put, proverbs are quoted, and many other literary matters are related and discussed. This institution is admirably adapted to cultivate the heads and to warm the hearts of an intelligent, generous people. Let me briefly describe the 'ceilidh' as I have seen it.

In a crofting townland there are several story-tellers who recite the oral literature of thier predecessors. The story-tellers of the Highlands are as varied in their subjects as are literary men and women elsewhere. One is a historian narrating events simply and concisely; another is a historian with a bias, colouring his narrative according to his leanings. One is an inventor, building fiction upon fact, mingling his materials, and investing the whole with the charm of novelty and the halo of romance. Another is a reciter of heroic poems and ballads, bringing the different characters before the mind as clearly as the sculptor brings the figure before the eye. One gives the songs of the chief poets, with interesting accounts of their authors, while another, generally a woman, sings, to weird airs, beautiful old songs, some of them Arthurian. There are various other narrators, singers, and speakers, but I have never heard aught that should not be said nor sung.

The romance school has the largest following, and I go there, joining others on the way. The house of the story-teller is already full, and it is difficult to get inside and away from the cold wind and soft sleet without. But with that politeness native to the people, the stranger is pressed to come forward and occupy the seat vacated for him beside the houseman. The house is roomy and clean, if homely, with its bright peat fire in the middle of the floor. There are many present—men and women, boys and girls. All the women are seated, and most of the men. Girls are crouched between the knees of fathers or brothers or friends, while boys are perched wherever—boy-like—they can climb.

The houseman is twisting twigs of heather into ropes to hold down thatch, a neighbour crofter is twining quicken roots into cords to tie cows, while another is plaiting bent grass into baskets to hold meal.

The housewife is spinning, a daughter is carding, another daughter is teazing, while a third daughter, supposed to be working, is away in the background conversing in low whispers with the son of a neighbouring crofter. Neighbour wives and neighbour daughters are knitting, sewing, or embroidering. The conversation is general: the local news, the weather, the price of cattle, these leading up to higher themes—the clearing of the glens (a sore subject), the war, the parliament, the effects of the sun upon the earth and the moon upon the tides.

The stranger asks the houseman to tell a story, and after a pause the man complies. The tale is full of incident, action, and pathos. It is told simply yet graphically, and at times dramatically—compelling the undivided attention of the listener. At the pathetic scenes and distressful events the bosoms of the women may be seen to heave and their silent tears to fall. Truth overcomes craft, skill conquers strength, and bravery is rewarded. Occasionally a momentary excitement occurs when heat and sleep overpower a boy and he tumbles down among the people below, to be trounced out and sent home. When the story is ended it is discussed and commented upon, and the different characters praised or blamed according to their merits and the views of the critics.

If not late, proverbs, riddles, conundrums, and songs follow. Some of the tales, however, are long, occupying a night or even several nights in recital.

The hut of Hector Macisaac, Ceannlangavat, South Uist, stood in a peat-moss. The walls were of turf, and the thatch of reeds, to the grief of the occupants, who looked upon the reed as banned, because it was used on Calvary to convey the sponge with the vinegar. The hut was about fifteen feet long, ten feet broad, and five feet high. There was nothing in it that the vilest thief in the lowest slum would condescend to steal. It were strange if the inmates of this turf hut in the peat-morass had been other than ailing. Hector Macisaac and his wife were the only occupants, their daughter being at service trying to prolong existence in her parents. Both had been highly endowed physically, and were still endowed mentally, though now advanced in years. The wife knew many secular runes, sacred hymns, and fairy songs; while the husband had numerous heroic tales, poems, and ballads.

I had visited these people before, and in September 1871 Iain F. Campbell of Islay and I went to see them. Hector Macisaac, the unlettered cottar who knew no language but his own, who came into contact with no one but those of his own class, his neighbours of the peat-bog, and who had never been out of his native island, was as polite and well-mannered and courteous as Iain Campbell, the learned barrister, the world-wide traveller, and the honoured guest of every court in Europe. Both were at ease and at home with one another, there being neither servility on the one side nor condescension on the other.

The stories and poems which Hector Macisaac went over during our visits to him would have filled several volumes. Mr Campbell now and then put a leading question which brought out the story-teller's marvellous memory and extensive knowledge of folklore.

It was similar with blind old Hector Macleod, cottar, Lianacuithe, South Uist, and with old Roderick Macneill, cottar, Miunghlaidh, Barra. Each of those men repeated stories and poems, tales and ballads, that would have filled many books. Yet neither of them told more than a small part of what he knew. None of the three men knew any letters, nor any language but Gaelic, nor had ever been out of his native island. All expressed regret in well-chosen words that they had not a better place in which to receive their visitors, and all thanked them in polite terms for coming to see them and for taking an interest in their decried and derided old lore. And all were courteous as the courtier.

During his visit to us, Mr Campbell expressed to my wife and to myself his admiration of these and other men with whom we had come in contact. He said that in no other race had he observed so many noble traits and high qualities as in the unlettered, untravelled, unspoiled Highlander.

In 1860, 1861, and 1862, I took down much folk-lore from Kenneth Morrison, cottar, Trithion, Skye. Kenneth Morrison had been a mason, but was now old, blind, and poor. Though wholly unlettered, he was highly intelligent. He mentioned the names of many old men in the extensive but now desolate parish of Minngnis, who had been famous story-tellers in his boyhood—men who had been born in the first decade of the eighteenth century. Several of these, he said, could recite stories and poems during many nights in succession—some of the tales requiring several nights to relate. He repeated fragments of many of these.

Kenneth Morrison told me that the old men, from whom he heard the poems and stories, said that they had heard them from old men in their boyhood. That would carry these old men back to the first half of the seventeenth century. Certainly they could not have learnt their stories or poems from books, for neither stories nor poems were printed in their time, and even had they been, those men could not have read them.

Gaelic oral literature has been disappearing during the last three centuries. It is now becoming meagre in quantity, inferior in quality, and greatly isolated.

Several causes have contributed towards this decadence—principally the Reformation, the Risings, the evictions, the Disruption, the schools, and the spirit of the age. Converts in religion, in politics, or in aught else, are apt to be intemperate in speech and rash in action. The Reformation movement condemned the beliefs and cults tolerated and assimilated by the Celtic Church and the Latin Church. Nor did sculpture and architecture escape their intemperate zeal. The risings harried and harassed the people, while the evictions impoverished, dispirited, and scattered them over the world. Ignorant school-teaching and clerical narrowness have been painfully detrimental to the expressive language, wholesome literature, manly sports, and interesting amusements of the Highland people. Innumerable examples occur.

A young lady said:—'When we came to Islay I was sent to the parish school to obtain a proper grounding in arithmetic. I was charmed with the schoolgirls and their Gaelic songs. But the schoolmaster—an alien like myself—denounced Gaelic speech and Gaelic songs. On getting out of school one evening the girls resumed a song they had been singing the previous evening. I joined willingly, if timidly, my knowledge of Gaelic being small. The schoolmaster heard us, however, and called us back. He punished us till the blood trickled from our fingers, although we were big girls, with the dawn of womanhood upon us. The thought of that scene thrills me with indignation.'

I was taking down a story from a man, describing how twin giants detached a huge stone from the parent rock, and how the two carried the enormous block of many tons upon their broad shoulders to lay it over a deep gully in order that their white-maned steeds might cross. Their enemy, however, came upon them in the night-time when thus engaged, and threw a magic mist around them, lessening their strength and causing them to fail beneath their burden. In the midst of the graphic description the grandson of the narrator, himself an aspirant teacher, called out in tones of superior authority, 'Grandfather, the teacher says that you ought to be placed upon the stool for your lying Gaelic stories.' The old man stopped and gasped in pained surprise. It required time and sympathy to soothe his feelings and to obtain the rest of the tale, which was wise, beautiful, and poetic, for the big, strong giants were Frost and Ice, and their subtle enemy was Thaw. The enormous stone torn from the parent rock is called 'Clach Mhor Leum nan Caorach,' the big stone of the leap of the sheep. Truly 'a little learning is a dangerous thing'! This myth was afterwards appreciated by the Royal Society of Edinburgh.

After many failures, and after going far to reach him, I induced a man to come to the lee of a knoll to tell me a tale. We were well into the spirit of the story when two men from the hill passed us. The story-teller hesitated, then stopped, saying that he would be reproved by his family, bantered by his friends, and censured by his minister.

Having made many attempts, I at last succeeded in getting a shepherd to come to me, in order to be away from his surroundings. The man travelled fifty-five miles, eight of these being across a stormy strait of the Atlantic. We had reached the middle of a tale when the sheriff of the district came to call on me in my rooms. The reciter fled, and after going more than a mile on his way home he met a man who asked him why he looked so scared, and why without his bonnet. The shepherd discovered that he had left his bonnet, his plaid, and his staff behind him in his flight. The remaining half of that fine story, as well as much other valuable Gaelic lore, died with the shepherd in Australia.

When Dr William Forbes Skene was preparing the third volume of *Celtic Scotland*, he asked me to write him a paper on the native system of holding the land, tilling the soil, and apportioning the stock in the Outer Hebrides. Being less familiar with Lewis than with the other portions of the Long Island, I visited Lewis again. It was with extreme difficulty that I could obtain any information on the subject of my inquiry, because it related to the foolish past rather than to the sedate present, to the secular affairs rather than to the religious life of the people. When I asked about old customs and old modes of working, I was answered, 'Good man, old things are passed away, all things are become new'; for the people of Lewis, like the people of the Highlands and Islands generally, carry the Scriptures in their minds and apply them in their speech as no other people do. It was extremely disconcerting to be met in this manner on a mission so desirable.

During my quest I went into a house near Ness. The house was clean and comfortable if plain and unpretending, most things in it being home-made. There were three girls in the house, young, comely, and shy, and four women, middle-aged, handsome, and picturesque in their homespun gowns and high-crowned mutches. Three of the women had been to the moorland pastures with their cattle, and had turned in here to rest on their way home.

'Hail to the house and household,' said I, greeting the inmates in the salutation of our fathers. 'Hail to you, kindly stranger,' replied the housewife. 'Come forward and take this seat. If it be not ill-mannered, may we ask whence you have come to-day? You are tired and travel-stained, and probably hungry?' 'I have come from Gress,' said I, 'round by Tolasta to the south, and Tolasta to the north, taking a look at the ruins of the Church of St Aula, at Gress, and at the ruins of the fort of Dunothail, and then across the moorland.' 'May the Posessor keep you in His own keeping, good man! You left early and have travelled far, and must be hungry.' With this the woman raised her eyes toward her daughters standing demurely silent, and motionless as Greek statues, in the background. In a moment the three fair girls became active and animated. One ran to the stack and brought in an armful of hard, black peats, another ran to the well and brought in a pail of clear spring water, while the third quickly spread a cloth, white as snow, upon the table in the inner room. The three neighbour women rose to leave, and I rose to do the same. 'Where are you going, good man?' asked the housewife in injured surprise, moving between me and the door. 'You must not go till you eat a bit and drink a sip. That indeed would be a reproach to us that we would not soon get over. These slips of lassies and I would not hear the end of it from the men at the sea, were we to allow a wayfarer to go from our door hungry, thirsty, and weary. No! no! you must not go till you eat a bite. Food will be ready presently, and in the meantime you will bathe your feet and dry your stockings, which are wet after coming through the marshes of the moorland.' Then the woman went down upon her knees, and washed and dried the feet of the stranger as gently and tenderly as a mother would those of her child. 'We have no stockings to suit the kilt,' said the woman in a tone of evident regret, 'but here is a pair of stockings of the houseman's which he has never had on, and perhaps you would put them on till your own are dry.'

One of the girls had already washed out my stockings, and they were presently drying before the bright fire on the middle of the floor. I deprecated all this trouble, but to no purpose. In an incredibly short time I was asked to go 'ben' and break bread.

The table was laden with wholesome food sufficient for several persons. There were fried herrings and boiled turbot fresh from the sea, and eggs fresh from the yard. There were fresh butter and salt butter, wheaten scones, barley bannocks, and oat cakes, with excellent tea, and cream. The woman apologised that she had no 'aran coinnich'—moss bread, that is, loaf bread—and no biscuits, they being simple crofter people far away from the big town.

'This,' said I, taking my seat, 'looks like the table for a betrothal, rather than for one man. Have you betrothals in Lewis?' I asked, turning my eyes towards the other room where we had left the three comely maidens. 'Oh, indeed, yes, the Lewis people are very good at marrying. Foolish young creatures, they often marry before they know their responsibilities or realise their difficulties,' and her eyes followed mine in the direction of her own young daughters. 'I suppose there is much fun and rejoicing at your marriages—music, dancing, singing, and merry-making of many kinds?' 'Oh, indeed, no, our weddings are now quiet and becoming, not the foolish things they were in my young days. In my memory weddings were great events, with singing and piping, dancing and amusements all night through, and generally for two and three nights in succession. Indeed, the feast of the kertch table, was almost as great as the feast of the marriage table, all the young men and maidens struggling to get to it. On the morning after the marriage the mother of the bride, and failing her the mother of the bridegroom, placed the three-cornered kertch, on the head of the bride before she rose from her bed. And the mother did this in name of the Sacred Three, under whose guidance the young wife was to walk. Then the bride arose and her maidens dressed her, and she came forth with the pointed kertch, on her head, and all the people present saluted her and shook hands with her, and the bards sang songs to her, and recited great rigmaroles, and there was much rejoicing and merrymaking all day long and all night through.

'There were many sad things done then, for those were the days of foolish doings and foolish people. Perhaps, on the day of the Lord, when they came out of church, if indeed they went into church, the young men would go to throw the stone, or to toss the cabar, or to play shinty, or to run races, or to race horses on the strand, the young maidens looking on the while, ay, and the old men and women.' 'And have you no music, no singing, no dancing now at your marriages?' 'May the Possessor keep you! I see that you are a stranger in Lewis, or you would not ask such a question,' the woman exclaimed with grief and surprise in her tone. 'It is long since we abandoned those foolish ways in Ness, and, indeed, throughout Lewis. In my young days there was hardly a house in Ness in which there was not one or two or three who could play the pipe, or the fiddle, or the trump. And I have heard it said that there were men, and women too, who could play things they called harps, and lyres, and bellow-pipes, but I do not know what those things were.' 'And why were those discontinued?' 'A blessed change came over the place and the people,' the woman replied in earnestness, 'and the good men and the good ministers who arose did away with the songs and the stories, the music and the dancing, the sports and the games, that were perverting the minds and ruining the souls of the people, leading them to folly and stumbling.' 'But how did the people themselves come to discard their sports and pastimes?' 'Oh, the good ministers and the good elders preached against them and went among the people, and besought them to forsake their follies and to return to wisdom. They made the people break and burn their pipes and fiddles. If there was a foolish man here and there who demurred, the good ministers and the good elders themselves broke and burnt their instruments.

'The people have forsaken their follies and their Sabbath-breaking, and there is no pipe, no fiddle here now,' said the woman in evident satisfaction. 'And what have you now instead of the racing, the stone-throwing, and the cabar-tossing, the song, the pipe, and the dance?' 'Oh, we have now the blessed Bible preached and explained to us faithfully and earnestly, if we sinful people would only walk in the right path and use our opportunities.'

'But what have you at your weddings? How do you pass the time?' 'Oh! the carles are on one side of the house talking of their crops and their nowt, and mayhap of the days when they were young and when things were different. And the young men are on the other side of the house talking about boats, and sailing, and militia, and naval reserve, perhaps of their own strength, and of many foolish matters besides.'

'And where are the girls? What are they doing?' 'Oh, they, silly things! are in the "culaist," back-house, perhaps trying to croon over some foolish song under their breath, perhaps trying to amble through some awkward steps of dancing on the points of their toes, or, shame to tell, perhaps speaking of what dress this or that girl had on at this or that marriage, or worse still, what hat this girl or that girl had on on the Day of the Lord, perhaps even on the Day of the Holy Communion, showing that their minds were on the vain things of the world instead of on the wise things of salvation.'

'But why are the girls in the "culaist"? What do they fear?'

'May the Good Being keep you, good man! They are in the "culaist" for concealment, and the fear of their life and of their death upon them, that they may be heard or seen should the good elder happen to be passing the way.' 'And should he, what then?' 'Oh, the elder will tell the minister, and the good minister will scold them from the pulpit, mentioning the girls by name. But the girls have a blanket on the door and another blanket on the window to deafen the sound and to obscure the light.'

'Do the young maidens allow the young men to join them in the "culaist"?' 'Indeed, truth to tell, the maidens would be glad enough to admit the young men were it not the fear of exposure. But the young men are so loud of voice, and so heavy of foot, and make so much noise, that they would betray the retreat of the girls, who would get rebuked, while the young men would escape. The girls would then be ashamed and downcast, and would not lift a head for a year and a day after their well-deserved scolding. They suffer most, for, sad to say, the young men are becoming less afraid of being admonished than they used to be.'

'And do the people have spirits at their marriages?' 'Oh yes, the minister is not so hard as that upon them at all. He does not interfere with them in that way unless they take too much, and talk loudly and quarrel. Then he is grieved and angry, and scolds them severely.'

'Perhaps were the minister to allow the people less drink and more music and dancing, singing and merry-making, they would enjoy it as much. I am sure the young girls would sing better, and dance better, with the help of the young men. And the young men themselves would be less loud of voice and less heavy of heel, among the maidens. Perhaps the happiness of the old people too, would be none the less real nor less lasting at seeing the joyousness of the young people.'

To this the woman promptly and loyally replied: 'The man of the Lord is untiring in work and unfailing in example for our good, and in guiding us to our heavenly home, constantly reminding us of the little-ness of time and the greatness of eternity, and he knows best, and we must do our best to follow his counsel and to imitate his example.'

A famous violin-player died in the island of Eigg a few years ago. He was known for his old style playing and his old-world airs which died with him. A preacher denounced him, saying—Thou art down there behind the door, thou miserable man with thy grey hair, playing thine old fiddle with the cold hand without, and the devil's fire within. His family pressed the man to burn his fiddle and never to play again. A pedlar came round and offered ten shillings for the violin. The instru-ment had been made by a pupil of Stradivarius, and was famed for its tone.—'It was not at all the thing that was got for it that grieved my heart so sorely, but the parting with it! the parting with it! and that I myself gave the best cow in my father's fold for it when I was young.' The voice of the old man faltered and a tear fell. He was never again seen to smile.

The reciters of religious lore were more rare and more reticent than the reciters of secular lore. Men and women whom I knew had hymns and incantations, but I did not know of this in time. The fragments

29

recalled by their families, like the fragments of Greek or Etruscan vases, indicated the originals.

Before dictating, the reciter went over the tale or poem, the writer making mental notes the while. This was helpful when, in the slow process of dictating, the narrator lost his thread and omitted passages. The poems were generally intoned in a low recitative manner, rising and falling in slow modulated cadences charming to hear but difficult to follow.

The music of the hymns had a distinct individuality, in some respects resembling and in many respects differing from the old Gregorian chants of the Church. I greatly regret that I was not able to record this peculiar and beautiful music, probably the music of the old Celtic Church.

Perhaps no people had a fuller ritual of song and story, of secular rite and religious ceremony, than the Highlanders. Mirth and music, song and dance, tale and poem, pervaded their lives, as electricity pervades the air. Religion, pagan or Christian, or both combined, permeated everything —blending and shading into one another like the iridescent colours of the rainbow. The people were sympathetic and synthetic, unable to see and careless to know where the secular began and the religious ended— an admirable union of elements in life for those who have lived it so truly and intensely as the Celtic races everywhere have done, and none more truly or more intensely than the ill-understood and so-called illiterate Highlanders of Scotland.

If this work does nothing else, it affords incontestable proof that the Northern Celts were endowed, as Renan justly claims for Celts everywhere, with 'profound feeling and adorable delicacy' in their religious instincts.[1]

The Celtic missionaries allowed the pagan stock to stand, grafting their Christian cult thereon. Hence the blending of the pagan and the Christian religions in these poems, which to many minds will constitute their chief charm. Gaelic lore is full of this blending and grafting—nor are they confined to the literature of the people, but extend indeed to

[1]*Poetry of the Celtic Races, and Other Studies.* By Ernest Renan.

30

their music, sculpture, and architecture. At Rodail, Harris, is a cruciform church of the thirteenth century. The church abuts upon a broad square tower of no great height. The tower is called 'Tur Chliamain,' tower of Clement, 'Claiman Mor Rodail,' Great Clement of Rodail. Tradition says that the tower is older than the church, and the masonry confirms the tradition.

There are sculptures within the church of much originality of design and of great beauty of execution, but the sculptures without are still more original and interesting. Round the sides of the square tower are the figures of birds and beasts, reptiles and fishes, and of men and women representing phallic worship. Here pagan cult joins with Christian faith, the East with the West, the past with the present. The traveller from India to Scotland can here see, on the cold, sterile rocks of Harris, the petrified symbols of a faith left living behind him on the hot, fertile plains of Hindustan. He can thus in his own person bridge over a space of eight thousand miles and a period of two thousand years.

There are observances and expressions current in the West which savour of the East, such as sun, moon, star, and fire worship, once prevalent, nor yet obsolete.

Highland divinities are full of life and action, local colour and individuality. These divinities filled the hearts and minds of the people of the Highlands, as their deities filled the hearts and minds of the people of Greece and Rome. The subject of these genii of the Highlands ought to be investigated and compared with those of other lands. Even yet, on the verge of disappearance, they would yield interesting results. Though loving their haunts and tenacious of their habitats, the genii of the Highlands are disappearing before the spirit of modernism, as the Red Indian, once bold and courageous, disappears before the white man. Once intrusive, they are now become timid as the mullet of the sea, the shrew of the grass, or the swift of the air—a glimpse, a glint, and gone for ever. They are startled at the crack of the rifle, the whistle of the steamer, the shriek of the train, and the click of the telegraph. Their homes are invaded and their repose is disturbed, so that they find no rest for their weary feet nor sleep for their heavy eyes; and their native land, so full of their love, so congenial to their hearts, will all too soon know them no

31

more. Let an attempt be made even yet to preserve their memories ere they disappear for ever.

Whatever be the value of this work, it is genuine folk-lore, taken down from the lips of men and women, no part being copied from books. It is the product of far-away thinking, come down on the long stream of time. Who the thinkers and whence the stream, who can tell? Some of the hymns may have been composed within the cloistered cells of Derry and Iona, and some of the incantations among the cromlechs of Stonehenge and the standing-stones of Callarnis. These poems were composed by the learned, but they have not come down through the learned, but through the unlearned—not through the lettered few, but through the unlettered many—through the crofters and cottars, the herdsmen and shepherds, of the Highlands and Islands.

Although these compositions have been rescued chiefly among Roman Catholics and in the islands, they have been equally common among Protestants and on the mainland.

From one to ten versions have been taken down, differing more or less. It has been difficult to select. Some examples of these variants are given. Several poems and many notes are wholly withheld, while a few of the poems and all the notes have been abbreviated for want of space.

With each succeeding generation Gaelic speech becomes more limited and Gaelic phraseology more obscure. Both reciter and writer felt this when words and phrases occurred which neither knew. These have been rendered tentatively or left untranslated. I can only hope that in the near or distant future some competent scholar may compare these gleanings of mine with Celtic writings at home and abroad, and that light may be shed upon what is to me obscure.

I have tried to translate literally yet satisfactorily, but I am painfully conscious of failure. Although in decay, these poems are in verse of a high order, with metre, rhythm, assonance, alliteration, and every quality to please the ear and to instruct the mind. The translation lacks these and the simple dignity, the charming grace, and the passionate devotion of the original. I see faults that I would willingly mend, but it is easier to point to blemishes than to avoid them.

Again and again I laid down my self-imposed task, feeling unable to render the intense power and supreme beauty of the original Gaelic into adequate English. But I resumed under the inspiring influence of my wife, to whose unfailing sympathy and cultured ear this work owes much.

My daughter has transcribed the manuscripts and corrected the proofs for press, and has acted as amanuensis throughout; while my three sons have helped in various ways.

The Celtic letters in the work have been copied by my wife from Celtic MSS., chiefly in the Advocates' Library. This has been a task of extreme difficulty, needing great skill and patient care owing to the defaced condition of the originals. The letters have been prepared for the engraver with feeling and insight by Mr John Athel Lovegrove, of H.M. Ordnance Survey.

My dear friend Mr George Henderson, M.A. Edin., Ph.D. Leipsic, B. Litt. Oxon., has helped and encouraged me throughout.

These, and the many others whose names I am unable to mention through want of space, I ask to accept my warm, abiding thanks.

Three sacrifices have been made—the sacrifice of time, the sacrifice of toil, and the sacrifice of means. These I do not regret. I have three regrets—that I had not been earlier collecting, that I have not been more diligent in collecting, and that I am not better qualified to treat what I have collected.

These notes and poems have been an education to me. And so have been the men and women reciters from whose dictation I wrote them down. They are almost all dead now, leaving no successors. With reverent hand and grateful heart I place this stone upon the cairn of those who composed and of those who transmitted the work.

ALEXANDER CARMICHAEL.

EDINBURGH,
St Michael's Day, 1899.

THE
INVOCATIONS

RUNE BEFORE PRAYER

Old people in the Isles sing this or some other short hymn before prayer. Sometimes the hymn and the prayer are intoned in low tremulous unmeasured cadences like the moving and moaning, the soughing and the sighing, of the ever-murmuring sea on their own wild shores.

They generally retire to a closet, to an outbuilding, to the lee of a knoll, or to the shelter of a dell, that they may not be seen nor heard of men. I have known men and women of eighty, ninety, and a hundred years of age continue the practice of their lives in going from one to two miles to the seashore to join their voices with the voicing of the waves and their praises with the praises of the ceaseless sea.

I am bending my knee
In the eye of the Father who created me,
In the eye of the Son who purchased me,
In the eye of the Spirit who cleansed me,
   In friendship and affection.
Through Thine own Anointed One, O God,
Bestow upon us fullness in our need,
    Love towards God,
    The affection of God,
    The smile of God,
    The wisdom of God,
    The grace of God,
    The fear of God,
    And the will of God
To do on the world of the Three,
As angels and saints
Do in heaven;
    Each shade and light,
    Each day and night,
    Each time in kindness,
    Give Thou us Thy Spirit.

THE CROSS OF THE SAINTS AND
THE ANGELS

THE cross of the saints and of the angels with me
From the top of my face to the edge of my soles.

      *   *   *   *   *

O Michael mild, O Mary of glory,
O gentle Bride of the locks of gold,
Preserve ye me in the weakly body,
The three preserve me on the just path.
    Oh! three preserve me on the just path.

Preserve ye me in the soul-shrine poor,
Preserve ye me, and I so weak and naked,
Preserve ye me without offence on the way,
The preservation of the three upon me to-night.
    Oh! the three to shield me to-night.

MORNING PRAYER

THANKS be to Thee, Jesus Christ,
Who brought'st me up from last night,
To the gladsome light of this day,
To win everlasting life for my soul,
Through the blood Thou didst shed for me.

Praise be to Thee, O God, for ever,
For the blessings Thou didst bestow on me—
My food, my speech, my work, my health,

   *   *   *   *

And I beseech Thee
To shield me from sin,
To shield me from ill,
To sain me this night,
And I low and poor,
O God of the poor!
O Christ of the wounds!
Give me wisdom along with Thy grace.

May the Holy One claim me,
And protect me on sea and on land,
And lead me on from step to step,
To the peace of the Everlasting City,
    The peace of the Everlasting City!

A PRAYER FOR GRACE

I AM bending my knee
In the eye of the Father who created me,
In the eye of the Son who died for me,
In the eye of the Spirit who cleansed me,
    In love and desire.

Pour down upon us from heaven
The rich blessing of Thy forgiveness;
Thou who art uppermost in the City,
    Be Thou patient with us.

Grant to us, Thou Saviour of Glory,
The fear of God, the love of God, and His affection,
And the will of God to do on earth at all times
As angels and saints do in heaven;
Each day and night give us Thy peace.
    Each day and night give us Thy peace.

THE GUIDING LIGHT OF ETERNITY

O GOD, who broughtst me from the rest of last night
Unto the joyous light of this day,
Be Thou bringing me from the new light of this day
Unto the guiding light of eternity.
Oh! from the new light of this day
Unto the guiding light of eternity.

HOUSE PROTECTING

GOD, bless the world and all that is therein.
God, bless my spouse and my children,
God, bless the eye that is in my head,
And bless, O God, the handling of my hand;
What time I rise in the morning early,
What time I lie down late in bed,
    Bless my rising in the morning early,
    And my lying down late in bed.

God, protect the house, and the household,
God, consecrate the children of the motherhood,
God, encompass the flocks and the young;
Be Thou after them and tending them,
What time the flocks ascend hill and wold,
What time I lie down to sleep,
    What time the flocks ascend hill and wold,
    What time I lie down in peace to sleep.

BLESS, O CHIEF OF GENEROUS CHIEFS

BLESS, O Chief of generous chiefs,
Myself and everything anear me,
Bless me in all my actions,
Make Thou me safe for ever,
    Make Thou me safe for ever.

From evey brownie and ban-shee,
From every evil wish and sorrow,
From every nymph and water-wraith,
From every fairy-mouse and grass-mouse,
    From every fairy-mouse and grass-mouse.

From every troll among the hills,
From every siren hard pressing me,
From every ghoul within the glens,
Oh! save me till the end of my day.
    Oh! save me till the end of my day.

THE DEDICATION

Thanks to Thee, God,
Who brought'st me from yesterday
To the beginning of to-day,
Everlasting joy
To earn for my soul
With good intent.
And for every gift of peace
Thou bestowest on me,
My thoughts, my words,
My deeds, my desires
I dedicate to Thee.
I supplicate Thee,
I beseech Thee,
To keep me from offence,
And to shield me to-night,
For the sake of Thy wounds
With Thine offering of grace.

BLESSING OF THE KINDLING

THE kindling of the fire is a work full of interest to the housewife. When 'lifting' the fire in the morning the woman prays, in an undertone, that the fire may be blessed to her and to her household, and to the glory of God who gave it. The people look upon fire as a miracle of Divine power provided for their good—to warm their bodies when they are cold, to cook their food when they are hungry, and to remind them that they too, like the fire, need constant renewal mentally and physically.

I WILL kindle my fire this morning
In presence of the holy angels of heaven,
In presence of Ariel of the loveliest form,
In presence of Uriel of the myriad charms,
Without malice, without jealousy, without envy,
Without fear, without terror of any one under the sun,
But the Holy Son of God to shield me.
> Without malice, without jealousy, without envy,
> Without fear, without terror of any one under the
>> sun,
> But the Holy Son of God to shield me.

God, kindle Thou in my heart within
A flame of love to my neighbour,
To my foe, to my friend, to my kindred all,
To the brave, to the knave, to the thrall,
O Son of the loveliest Mary,
From the lowliest thing that liveth,
To the Name that is highest of all.
> O Son of the loveliest Mary,
> From the lowliest thing that liveth,
> To the Name that is highest of all.

GIVE THY MILK

THE milking songs of the people are numerous and varied. They are sung to pretty airs, to please the cows and to induce them to give their milk. The cows become accustomed to these lilts and will not give their milk without them, nor, occasionally, without their favourite airs being sung to them. This fondness of Highland cows for music induces owners of large herds to secure milkmaids possessed of good voices and some 'go.' It is interesting and animating to see three or four comely girls among a fold of sixty, eighty, or a hundred picturesque Highland cows on meadow or mountain slope. The moaning and heaving of the sea afar, the swish of the wave on the shore, the carolling of the lark in the sky, the unbroken song of the mavis on the rock, the broken melody of the merle in the brake, the lowing of the kine without, the response of the calves within the fold, the singing of the milkmaids in unison with the movement of their hands, and of the soft sound of the snowy milk falling into the pail, the gilding of hill and dale, the glowing of the distant ocean beyond, as the sun sinks into the sea of golden glory, constitute a scene which the observer would not, if he could, forget.

GIVE thy milk, brown cow,
Give thy milk, brown cow,
Give thy milk, brown cow,
   Heavily flowing.

My beloved shall get white-bellied calves,
And a fetter fine that shall go kindly round her legs;
No fetter of hair, nor of heather, nor of lint refuse,
But a dear fetter that men bring from Saxon land.
    Oh! ho! from Saxon land.

And my queen maiden of beauty shall get
A fetter smooth to go softly round her legs;
No fetter of cord, nor of lint, nor lint refuse,
But a fetter of silk up from Saxon land.
    Oh! ho! from Saxon land.

My beloved shall get grass and shelter,
She shall get hill, heath, and plain,
She shall get meadow-grass, club-rush, and stubble,
And she shall get the wine that comes from the elements of
      the steep bens.
    Oh! ho! the steep bens.

HO, MY HEIFER!

THE night the Herdsman was out
No shackle went on a cow,
Lowing ceased not from the mouth of calf
Wailing the Herdsman of the flock,
    Wailing the Herdsman of the flock.

    Ho my heifer! ho my heifer!
    Ho my heifer! my heifer beloved!
My heartling heart, kind, fond,
For the sake of the High King take to thy calf.

The night the Herdsman was missing,
In the Temple He was found.
The King of the moon to come hither!
The King of the sun down from heaven!
    King of the sun down from heaven!

RULER OF THE ELEMENTS

THE Children of Israel, God taking them,
    Through the Red Sea obtained a path,
They obtained the quenching of their thirst
    From a rock that might not by craftsman be hewn.

Who are they on the tiller of my rudder,
    Giving speed to my east bound barge?
Peter and Paul and John the beloved,
    Three to whom laud and obeisance are due.

Who are the group near to my helm?
    Peter and Paul and John the Baptist;
Christ is sitting on my helm,
    Making guidance to the wind from the south.

To whom does tremble the voice of the wind?
    To whom become tranquil strait and ocean?
To Jesus Christ, Chief of each saint,
    Son of Mary, Root of victory,
    Son of Mary, Root of victory.

JESU, THOU SON OF MARY

Jesu, Thou Son of Mary,
Have mercy upon us,
    Amen.
Jesu, Thou Son of Mary,
Make peace with us,
    Amen.
Oh, with us and for us
Where we shall longest be,
    Amen.
Be about the morning of our course,
Be about the closing of our life,
    Amen.
Be at the dawning of our life,
And oh! at the dark'ning of our day,
    Amen.
Be for us and with us,
Merciful God of all,
    Amen.

Consecrate us
Condition and lot,
Thou King of kings,
Thou God of all,
    Amen.

Consecrate us
Rights and means,
Thou King ot kings,
Thou God of all,
                    Amen.
Consecrate us
Heart and body,
Thou King of kings,
Thou God of all,
                    Amen.
Each heart and body,
Each day to Thyself,
Each night accordingly,
Thou King of kings,
Thou God of all,
                    Amen.

HERDING BLESSING

BEING a pastoral people, the Highlanders possess much pastoral poetry. The greater part of this is secular with fragments of sacred poetry interspersed. The herding runes are examples of these purely pastoral poems. They are sung by the people as they send their flocks to the pastures, or tend them on the hills, glens, or plains. The customs vary in details in different districts, but everywhere is the simple belief that the King of shepherds watches over men and flocks now as of old—'the same yesterday, to-day, and for ever.'

I WILL place this flock before me,
As was ordained of the King of the world,
Bride to keep them, to watch them, to tend them,
On ben, on glen, on plain,
    Bride to keep them, to watch them, to tend them,
    On ben, on glen, on plain.

Arise, thou Bride the gentle, the fair,
Take thou thy lint, thy comb, and thy hair,
Since thou to them madest the noble charm,
To keep them from straying, to save them from harm,
    Since thou to them madest the noble charm,
    To keep them from straying, to save them from harm.

From rocks, from drifts, from streams,
From crooked passes, from destructive pits,
From the straight arrows of the slender ban-shee,
From the heart of envy, from the eye of evil,
    From the straight arrows of the slender ban-shee,
    From the heart of envy, from the eye of evil.

Mary Mother, tend thou the offspring all,
Bride of the fair palms, guard thou my flocks,
Kindly Columba, thou saint of many powers,
Encompass thou the breeding cows, bestow on me herds,
    Kindly Columba, thou saint of many powers,
    Encompass thou the breeding cows, bestow on me
        herds.

THE PROTECTION OF THE CATTLE

PASTURES smooth, long, and spreading,
Grassy meads aneath your feet,
The friendship of God the Son to bring you home
To the field of the fountains,
    Field of the fountains.

Closed be every pit to you,
Smoothed be every knoll to you,
Cosy every exposure to you,
Beside the cold mountains,
    Beside the cold mountains.

The care of Peter and Paul,
The care of James and of John,
The care of Bride fair and of Mary Virgin,
To meet you and to tend you,
    Oh! the care of all the band
    To protect you and to strengthen you.

GOD WITH ME LYING DOWN

THIS poem was taken down in 1866 from Mary Macrae, Harris. She often walked with companions, after the work of the day was done, distances of ten and fifteen miles to a dance, and after dancing all night walked back again to the work of the morning fresh and vigorous as if nothing unusual had occurred.

The people of Harris had been greatly given to old lore and to the old ways of their fathers, reciting and singing, dancing and merry-making; but a reaction occurred, and Mary Macrae's old-world ways were abjured and condemned.

But Mary Macrae heeded not, and went on in her own way, singing her songs and ballads, intoning her hymns and incantations, and chanting her own mouth music, and dancing to her own shadow when nothing better was available.

GOD with me lying down,
God with me rising up,
God with me in each ray of light,
Nor I a ray of joy without Him,
    Nor one ray without Him.

Christ with me sleeping,
Christ with me waking,
Christ with me watching,
Every day and night,
    Each day and night.

God with me protecting,
The Lord with me directing,
The Spirit with me strengthening,
For ever and for evermore,
    Ever and evermore, Amen.
    Chief of chiefs, Amen.

JESU WHO OUGHT TO BE PRAISED

THE reciter said that this poem was composed by a woman in Harris. She was afflicted with leprosy, and was removed from the community on the upland to dwell alone on the sea-shore, where she lived on the plants of the plains and on the shell-fish of the strand. It is told that all her sores became healed and her flesh became new.

In a similar way, many lepers who came to the shrine of St. James in Compostela in Spain during the Middle Ages, were said to have been healed by eating fish and shell-fish from the bay of Compostela.

 IT were as easy for Jesu
To renew the withered tree
As to wither the new
Were it His will so to do.
    Jesu! Jesu! Jesu!
    Jesu! meet it were to praise Him.

There is no plant in the ground
But is full of His virtue,
There is no form in the strand
But is full of His blessing.
    Jesu! Jesu! Jesu!
    Jesu! meet it were to praise Him.

There is no life in the sea,
There is no creature in the river,
There is naught in the firmament,
But proclaims His goodness.
    Jesu! Jesu! Jesu!
    Jesu! meet it were to praise Him.

There is no bird on the wing,
There is no star in the sky,
There is nothing beneath the sun,
But proclaims His goodness.
    Jesu! Jesu! Jesu!
    Jesu! meet it were to praise Him.

THE CLIPPING BLESSING

When a man has shorn a sheep and has set it free, he waves his hand after it and blesses it. In the case of this blessing it must be a ewe, for he tells it to bear a female lamb for the feast of Beltane, the first of May.

Go shorn and come woolly,
Bear the Beltane female lamb,
Be the lovely Bride thee endowing,
And the fair Mary thee sustaining,
    The fair Mary sustaining thee.

Michael the chief be shielding thee
From the evil dog and from the fox,
From the wolf and from the sly bear,
And from the taloned birds of destructive bills,
    From the taloned birds of hooked bills.

THE QUERN BLESSING ON ASH EVE

A QUERN is used for grinding grain into flour.

WE shall have mead,
We shall have spruce,
We shall have wine,
We shall have feast.
We shall have sweetness and milk produce,
Honey and milk,
Wholesome ambrosia,
Abundance of that,
Abundance of that.

We shall have harp,
We shall have harp,
We shall have lute,
We shall have horn.
We shall have sweet psaltery
Of the melodious strings
And the regal lyre,
Of the songs we shall have,
Of the songs we shall have.

And the King of kings
And Jesus Christ,
And the Spirit of peace
And of grace be with us,
Of grace be with us.

THE CONSECRATION OF THE SEED

THE corn is prepared at certain seasons of the year, which are seldom deviated from. The rye is threshed to allow the soft wind of November and December to winnow the seed; the oats to allow the cold winds of January and February to winnow the seed; and the bere (barley) to allow the sharp winds of March and April, to winnow the seed. All these preparations are made to assist Nature in the coming Spring. Three days before being sown the seed is sprinkled with clear cold water, in the name of Father, and of Son, and of Spirit, the person sprinkling the seed walking sunwise the while.

The ritual is picturesque, and is performed with great care and solemnity and, like many of these ceremonies, is a combination of Paganism and Christianity.

I WILL go out to sow the seed,
In name of Him who gave it growth;
I will place my front in the wind,
And throw a gracious handful on high.
Should a grain fall on a bare rock,
It shall have no soil in which to grow;
As much as falls into the earth,
The dew will make it to be full.

Friday, day auspicious,
The dew will come down to welcome
Every seed that lay in sleep
Since the coming of cold without mercy;
Every seed will take root in the earth,
As the King of the elements desired,
The braird will come forth with the dew,
It will inhale life from the soft wind.

I will come round with my step,
I will go rightways with the sun,
In name of Ariel and the angels nine,
In name of Gabriel and the Apostles kind.
Father, Son, and Spirit Holy,
Be giving growth and kindly substance
To every thing that is in my ground,
Till the day of gladness shall come.

The Feast day of Michael, day beneficent,
I will put my sickle round about
The root of my corn as was wont;
I will lift the first cut quickly;
I will put it three turns round
My head, saying my rune the while,
My back to the airt of the north;
My face to the fair sun of power.

I shall throw the handful far from me,
I shall close my two eyes twice,
Should it fall in one bunch
My stacks will be productive and lasting;
No Carlin will come with bad times
To ask a palm bannock from us,
What time rough storms come with frowns
Nor stint nor hardship shall be on us.

GOD BE WITH US

 GOD be with us
On this Thy day,

   Amen.

[God be with us
On this Thy night,

   Amen.]

To us and with us,
On this Thy day,

   Amen.

[To us and with us,
On this Thy night,

   Amen.]

It is clear to be seen of us,
Since we came into the world,
That we have deserved Thy wrath,

   Amen.

O Thine own wrath,
Thou God of all,

   Amen.

Grant us forgiveness,

   Amen.

Grant us forgiveness,
                    Amen.
Grant to us Thine own forgiveness,
Thou merciful God of all,
                    Amen.
Anything that is evil to us,
Or that may witness against us
Where we shall longest be,
Illume it to us,
Obscure it to us,
Banish it from us,
Root it out of our hearts,
Ever, evermore, everlastingly.
        Ever, evermore, everlastingly.
                    Amen.

REAPING BLESSING

THE day the people began to reap the corn was a day of commotion and ceremonial in the townland. The whole family repaired to the field dressed in their best attire to hail the God of the harvest.

Laying his bonnet on the ground, the father of the family took up his sickle, and facing the sun, he cut a handful of corn. Putting the handful of corn three times sunwise round his head, the man raised the reaping salutation. The whole family took up the strain and praised the God of the harvest, who gave them corn and bread, food and flocks, wool and clothing, health and strength, and peace and plenty.

When the reaping was finished the people had a trial called casting the sickles, and trial of hooks. This consisted, among other things, of throwing the sickles high up in the air, and observing how they came down, how each struck the earth, and how it lay on the ground. From these observations the people augured who was to remain single and who was to be married, who was to be sick and who was to die, before the next reaping came round.

 GOD, bless Thou Thyself my reaping,
Each ridge, and plain, and field,
Each sickle curved, shapely, hard,
Each ear and handful in the sheaf,
    Each ear and handful in the sheaf.

Bless each maiden and youth,
Each woman and tender youngling,
Safeguard them beneath Thy shield of strength,
And guard them in the house of the saints,
    Guard them in the house of the saints.

Encompass each goat, sheep and lamb,
Each cow and horse, and store,
Surround Thou the flocks and herds,
And tend them to a kindly fold,
    Tend them to a kindly fold.

For the sake of Michael head of hosts,
Of Mary fair-skinned branch of grace,
Of Bride smooth-white of ringleted locks,
Of Columba of the graves and tombs,
    Columba of the graves and tombs.

REAPING BLESSING

THE word "airt" means direction.

ON Tuesday of the feast at the rise of the sun,
And the back of the ear of corn to the east,
I will go forth with my sickle under my arm,
And I will reap the cut the first act.

I will let my sickle down
While the fruitful ear is in my grasp,
I will raise mine eye upwards,
I will turn me on my heel quickly,

Rightway as travels the sun
From the airt of the east to the west,
From the airt of the north with motion calm
To the very core of the airt of the south.

I will give thanks to the King of grace
For the growing crops of the ground,
He will give food to ourselves and to the flocks
According as He disposeth to us.

James and John, Peter and Paul,
Mary beloved, the fullness of light,

       *   *   *   *

       *   *   *   *

On Michaelmas Eve and Christmas,
We will all taste of the bannock.

BRIDE THE MIDWIFE

THERE came to me assistance,
Mary fair and Bride;
As Anna bore Mary,
As Mary bore Christ,
As Eile bore John the Baptist
Without flaw in him,
Aid thou me in mine unbearing,
   Aid me, O Bride!

As Christ was conceived of Mary
Full perfect on every hand,
Assist thou me, foster-mother,
The conception to bring from the bone;
And as thou didst aid the Virgin of joy,
Without gold, without corn, without kine,
Aid thou me, great is my sickness,
   Aid me, O Bride!

LOOM BLESSING

In the Outer Isles women generally do the weaving, while in the Inner Isles and on the mainland it is usually done by men.

In Uist, when the woman stops weaving on Saturday night she carefully ties up her loom and suspends the cross or crucifix above the sleay. This is for the purpose of keeping away the brownie, the banshee, the 'peallan,' and all evil spirits and malign influences from disarranging the thread and the loom. And all this is done with loving care and in good faith, and in prayer and purity of heart.

BLESS, O Chief of generous chiefs,
My loom and everything a-near me,
Bless me in my every action,
Make Thou me safe while I live.

From every brownie and fairy woman,
From every evil wish and sorrow,
Help me, O Thou helping Being,
As long as I shall be in the land of the living.

In name of Mary, mild of deeds,
In name of Columba, just and potent,
Consecrate the four posts of my loom,
Till I begin on Monday.

Her pedals, her sleay, and her shuttle,
Her reeds, her warp, and her cogs,
Her cloth-beam, and her thread-beam,
Thrums and the thread of the plies.

68

Every web, black, white, and fair,
Roan, dun, checked, and red,
Give Thy blessing everywhere,
On every shuttle passing under the thread.

Thus will my loom be unharmed,
Till I shall arise on Monday;
Beauteous Mary will give me of her love,
And there shall be no obstruction I shall not overcome.

LOOM BLESSING

THRUMS nor odds of thread
My hand never kept, nor shall keep,

Every colour in the bow of the shower
Has gone through my fingers beneath the cross,

White and black, red and madder,
Green, dark grey, and scarlet,

Blue, and roan, and colour of the sheep,
And never a particle of cloth was wanting.

I beseech calm Bride the generous,
I beseech mild Mary the loving,
I beseech Christ Jesu the humane,
That I may not die without them,
　　That I may not die without them.

DESIRES

MAY I speak each day according to Thy justice,
Each day may I show Thy chastening, O God;
May I speak each day according to Thy wisdom,
Each day and night may I be at peace with Thee.

Each day may I count the causes of Thy mercy,
May I each day give heed to Thy laws;
Each day may I compose to Thee a song,
May I harp each day Thy praise, O God.

May I each day give love to Thee, Jesu,
Each night may I do the same;
Each day and night, dark and light,
May I laud Thy goodness to me, O God.

HOLY FATHER OF GLORY

THANKS be to Thee, Holy Father of Glory,
Father kind, ever-loving, ever-powerful,
Because of all the abundance, favour, and deliverance
That Thou bestowest upon us in our need.
Whatever providence befalls us as thy children,
In our portion, in our lot, in our path,
Give to us with it the rich gifts of Thine hand
And the joyous blessing of Thy mouth.

We are guilty and polluted, O God,
In spirit, in heart, and in flesh,
In thought, in word, in act,
We are hard in Thy sight in sin.
Put Thou forth to us the power of Thy love,
Be thou leaping over the mountains of our transgressions,
And wash us in the true blood of conciliation,
Like the down of the mountain, like the lily of the lake.

In the steep common path of our calling,
Be it easy or uneasy to our flesh,
Be it bright or dark for us to follow,
Thine own perfect guidance be upon us.
Be Thou a shield to us from the wiles of the deceiver,
From the arch-destroyer with his arrows pursuing us,
And in each secret thought our minds get to weave,
Be Thou Thyself on our helm and at our sheet.

Though dogs and thieves would reive us from the fold,
Be Thou the valiant Shepherd of glory near us.
Whatever matter or cause or propensity,
That would bring to us grief, or pains, or wounds,
Or that would bear witness against us at the last,
On the other side of the great river of dark shadows,
Oh! do Thou obscure it from our eyes,
And from our hearts drive it for ever.

Now to the Father who created each creature,
Now to the Son who paid ransom for His people,
Now to the Holy Spirit, Comforter of might:—
Shield and sain us from every wound;
Be about the beginning and end of our race,
Be giving us to sing in glory,
In peace, in rest, in reconciliation,
Where no tear shall be shed, where death comes no more.
　　Where no tear shall be shed, where death comes no more.

PRAYER FOR TRAVELLING

THIS hymn was sung by a pilgrim in setting out on his pilgrimage. The family and friends joined the traveller in singing the hymn and starting the journey, from which too frequently, for various causes, he never returned.

LIFE be in my speech,
Sense in what I say,
The bloom of cherries on my lips,
Till I come back again.

The love Christ Jesus gave
Be filling every heart for me,
The love Christ Jesus gave
Filling me for every one.

Traversing corries, traversing forests,
Traversing valleys long and wild.
The fair white Mary still uphold me,
The Shepherd Jesu be my shield,
The fair white Mary still uphold me,
The Shepherd Jesu be my shield.

GOD GUIDE ME

God guide me with Thy wisdom,
God chastise me with Thy justice,
God help me with Thy mercy,
God protect me with Thy strength.

God fill me with Thy fullness,
God shield me with Thy shade,
God fill me with Thy grace,
For the sake of Thine Anointed Son.

Jesu Christ of the seed of David,
Visiting One of the Temple,
Sacrificial Lamb of the Garden,
Who died for me.

HUNTING BLESSING

A YOUNG man was consecrated before he went out to hunt. Oil was put on his head, a bow was placed in his hand, and he was required to stand with bare feet on the bare grassless ground. The dedication of the young hunter was akin to those of the judge, the chief, and the king, on installation. Many conditions were imposed on the young man, which he was required to observe throughout life. He was not to take life wantonly. He was not to kill a bird sitting, nor a beast lying down, and he was not to kill the mother of a brood, nor the mother of a suckling. Nor was he to kill an unfledged bird nor a suckling beast, unless it might be the young of a bird, or of a beast, of prey. It was at all times permissible and laudable to destroy certain clearly defined birds and beasts of prey and evil reptiles, with their young.

FROM my loins begotten wert thou, my son,
May I guide thee the way that is right,
In the holy name of the apostles eleven
In name of the Son of God torn of thee.

In name of James, and Peter, and Paul,
John the baptist, and John the apostle above,
Luke the physician, and Stephen the martyr,
Muriel the fair, and Mary mother of the Lamb.

In name of Patrick holy of the deeds,
And Carmac of the rights and tombs,
Columba beloved, and Adamnan of laws,
Fite calm, and Bride of the milk and kine.

In name of Michael chief of hosts,
In name of Ariel youth of lovely hues,
In name of Uriel of the golden locks,
And Gabriel seer of the Virgin of grace.

The time thou shalt have closed thine eye,
Thou shalt not bend thy knee nor move,
Thou shalt not wound the duck that is swimming,
Never shalt thou harry her of her young.

The white swan of the sweet gurgle,
The speckled dun of the brown tuft,
Thou shalt not cut a feather from their backs,
Till the doom-day, on the crest of the wave.

On the wing be they always
Ere thou place missile to thine ear,
And the fair Mary will give thee of her love,
And the lovely Bride will give thee of her kine.

Thou shalt not eat fallen fish nor fallen flesh,
Nor one bird that thy hand shall not bring down,
Be thou thankful for the one,
Though nine should be swimming.

The fairy swan of Bride of flocks,
The fairy duck of Mary of peace.

FISHING BLESSING

THE people of Uist say that the haddock was the fish in whose mouth Peter found the tribute-money, and that the two black spots are the marks left by Peter's fingers when he held the fish to extract the money from its mouth. The crew of young men who get most haddocks on Christmas Day are looked upon during the year as the real followers of the king of fishers. There is, therefore, considerable emulation among the different crews.

The haddock is called Peter's fish, and a family of birds Peter-like, petrels, because in their flight they seem to be walking on the sea.

 THE day of light has come upon us,
Christ is born of the Virgin.

In His name I sprinkle the water
Upon every thing within my court.

Thou King of deeds and powers above,
Thy fishing blessing pour down on us.

I will sit me down with an oar in my grasp,
I will row me seven hundred and seven strokes.

I will cast down my hook,
The first fish which I bring up

In the name of Christ, King of the elements,
The poor shall have it at his wish.

And the king of fishers, the brave Peter,
He will after it give me his blessing.

Ariel, Gabriel, and John,
Raphael benign, and Paul,

Columba, tender in every distress,
And Mary fair, the endowed of grace.

Encompass ye us to the fishing-bank of ocean,
And still ye to us the crest of the waves.

Be the King of kings at the end of our course,
Of lengthened life and of lasting happiness.

Be the crown of the King from the Three on high,
Be the cross of Christ adown to shield us,
    The crown of the King from the Three above,
    The cross of Christ adown to shield us.

THE NEW MOON

THIS little prayer is said by old men and women in the islands of Barra. When they first see the new moon they make their obeisance to it as to a great chief. The women curtsey gracefully and the men bow low, raising their bonnets reverently. The bow of the men is peculiar, partaking somewhat of the curtsey of the women, the left knee being bent and the right drawn forward towards the middle of the left leg in a curious but not inelegant manner.

The fragment of moon-worship is now a matter of custom rather than of belief, although it exists over the whole British Isles.

In Cornwall the people nod to the new moon and turn silver in their pockets. In Edinburgh cultured men and women turn the rings on their fingers and make their wishes. A young English lady told the writer that she had always been in the habit of bowing to the new moon, till she had been bribed out of it by her father, a clergyman, putting money in her pocket lest her lunar worship should compromise him with his bishop. She naïvely confessed, however, that among the free mountains of Loch Etive she reverted to the good customs of her fathers, from which she derived great satisfaction!

IN name of the Holy Spirit of grace,
In name of the Father of the City of peace,
In name of Jesus who took death off us,
Oh! in name of the Three who shield us in every need,
If well thou hast found us to-night,
Seven times better mayest thou leave us without harm,
    Thou bright white Moon of the seasons,
    Bright white Moon of the seasons.

THE DAY OF ST COLUMBA

THURSDAY was St. Columba's Day—and through him the day of many important events in the economy of the people. It was a lucky day for all enterprises—for warping thread, for beginning a pilgrimage, or any other undertaking.

Maunday Thursday is called in Uist 'Gruel Thursday,' and in Iona 'Great Gruel Thursday.' On this day people in maritime districts made offerings of mead, ale, or gruel to the god of the sea. As the day merged from Wednesday to Thursday a man walked to the waist into the sea and poured out whatever offering had been prepared, chanting:—

> O God of the sea,
> Put weed in the drawing wave
> To enrich the ground,
> To shower on us food.

Those behind the offerer took up the chant and wafted it along the sea-shore on the midnight air, the darkness of night and the rolling of the waves making the scene weird and impressive.

THURSDAY of Columba benign,
Day to send sheep on prosperity,
Day to send cow on calf,
Day to put the web in the warp.

Day to put coracle on the brine,
Day to place the staff to the flag,
Day to bear, day to die,
Day to hunt the heights.

Day to put horses in harness,
Day to send herds to pasture,
Day to make prayer efficacious,
Day of my beloved, the Thursday,
    Day of my beloved, the Thursday.

THE OCEAN BLESSING

 O THOU who pervadest the heights,
Imprint on us Thy gracious blessing,
Carry us over the surface of the sea,
Carry us safely to a haven of peace,
Bless our boatmen and our boat,
Bless our anchors and our oars,
Each stay and halyard and traveller,
Our mainsails to our tall masts
Keep, O King of the elements, in their place
That we may return home in peace;
I myself will sit down at the helm,
It is God's own Son who will give me guidance,
As He gave to Columba the mild
What time he set stay to sails.

Mary, Bride, Michael, Paul,
Peter, Gabriel, John of love,
Pour ye down from above the dew
That would make our faith to grow,
Establish ye us in the Rock of rocks,
In every law that love exhibits,
That we may reach the land of glory,
Where peace and love and mercy reign,
All vouchsafed to us through grace;
Never shall the canker worm get near us,
We shall there be safe for ever,
We shall not be in the bonds of death
Though we are of the seed of Adam.

On the Feast Day of Michael, the Feast Day of Martin,
The Feast Day of Andrew, band of mercy,
The Feast Day of Bride, day of my choice,
Cast ye the serpent into the ocean,
So that the sea may swallow her up;
On the Feast Day of Patrick, day of power,
Reveal to us the storm from the north,
Quell its wrath and blunt its fury,
Lessen its fierceness, kill its cold.

On the Day of the Three Kings on high,
Subdue to us the crest of the waves,
On Beltane Day give us the dew,
On John's Day the gentle wind,
The Day of Mary the great of fame,
Ward off us the storm from the west;
Each day and night, storm and calm,
Be Thou with us, O Chief of chiefs,
Be Thou Thyself to us a compass-chart,
Be Thine hand on the helm of our rudder,
Thine own hand, Thou God of the elements,
Early and late as is becoming,
　　Early and late as is becoming.

CHRISTMAS HAIL

CHRISTMAS chants were numerous and their recital common throughout Scotland. They are now disappearing with the customs they accompanied. Where they still linger their recital is relegated to boys. Formerly on Christmas Eve bands of young men went about from house to house and from townland to townland chanting Christmas songs. The singers wore long white shirts for surplices, and very tall white hats for mitres, in which they made a picturesque appearance as they moved along singing their loudest. Sometimes they went about as one band, sometimes in sections of twos and threes. When they entered a dwelling they took possession of a child, if there was one in the house. The child was called Little Christ. The assumed Christ was placed on a skin, and carried three times round the fire, sunwise, by the head of the band, the song men singing the Christmas Hail. The skin on which the symbolic Christ was carried was that of a white male lamb without spot or blemish and consecrated to this service. The skin was called 'uilim.' Homage and offerings and much rejoicing were made to the symbolic Christ. The people of the house gave the singers bread, butter, crowdie, and other eatables, on which they afterwards feasted.

The poem which follows was taken down from Angus Gunn, Ness, Lewis, then over eighty-four years of age. Angus Gunn had been a strong man physically and was still a strong man mentally. He had lived for many years in the island of North Roney, and gave a graphic description of it, and of his life there. Roney is a small, precipitous island in the North Atlantic, sixty miles from the Butt of Lewis and sixty miles from Cape Wrath, forming the apex of a triangle between the two promontories. It is inaccessible except in a smooth sea, which is rare there. The island is now uninhabited.

HAIL King! hail King! blessed is He! blessed is He!
Hail King! hail King! blessed is He! blessed is He!
Hail King! hail King! blessed is He,
    the King of whom we sing,
      All hail! let there be joy!

This night is the eve of the great Nativity,
Born is the Son of Mary the Virgin,
The soles of His feet have reached the earth,
The Son of glory down from on high,
Heaven and earth glowed to Him,
      All hail! let there be joy!

The peace of earth to Him, the joy of heaven to Him,
Behold His feet have reached the world;
The homage of a King be His, the welcome of a Lamb be His,
King all victorious, Lamb all glorious,
Earth and ocean illumed to Him,
      All hail! let there be joy!

The mountains glowed to Him, the plains glowed to Him,
The voice of the waves with the song of the strand,
Announcing to us that Christ is born,
Son of the King of kings from the land of salvation;
Shone the sun on the mountains high to Him,
      All hail! let there be joy!

Shone to Him the earth and sphere together,
God the Lord has opened a Door;
Son of Mary Virgin, hasten Thou to help me,
Thou Christ of hope, Thou Door of joy,
Golden Sun of hill and mountain,
        All hail! let there be joy!

Offer to the Being from found to cover,
Include stave and stone and beam;
Offer again both rods and cloth,
Be health to the people therein,
    Hail King! hail King! blessed is He! blessed is He!
    Hail King! hail King! blessed is He! blessed is He!
       Ho, hail! blessed the King!
          Let there be joy!

       Blessed the King,
       Without beginning, without ending,
       To everlasting, to eternity,
          Every generation for aye,
          Ho! hi! let there be joy!

THE SHEPHERD OF THE FLOCK
WAS BORN

THAT night the star shone
Was born the Shepherd of the Flock,
Of the Virgin of the hundred charms,
    The Mary Mother.

The Trinity eternal by her side,
In the manger cold and lowly.
Come and give tithes of thy means
    To the Healing Man.

The foam-white breastling beloved,
Without one home in the world,
The tender holy Babe forth driven,
    Immanuel!

Ye three angels of power,
Come ye, come ye down;
To the Christ of the people
    Give ye salutation.

Kiss ye His hands,
Dry ye His feet
With the hair of your heads;
And O! Thou world-pervading God,
And Ye, Jesu, Michael, Mary,
    Do not Ye forsake us.

HEY THE GIFT, HO THE GIFT

HEY the Gift, ho the Gift,
Hey the Gift, on the living.

Son of the dawn, Son of the clouds,
Son of the planet, Son of the star,
Hey the Gift, ho the Gift,
Hey the Gift, on the living.

Son of the rain, Son of the dew,
Son of the welkin, Son of the sky,
Hey the Gift, ho the Gift,
Hey the Gift, on the living.

Son of the flame, Son of the light,
Son of the sphere, Son of the globe,
Hey the Gift, ho the Gift,
Hey the Gift, on the living.

Son of the elements, Son of the heavens,
Son of the moon, Son of the sun,
      Hey the Gift, ho the Gift,
      Hey the Gift, on the living.

Son of Mary of the God-mind,
And the Son of God first of all news,
      Hey the Gift, ho the Gift,
      Hey the Gift, on the living.

THE GIFTS OF THE THREE

Spirit, give me of Thine abundance,
Father, give me of Thy wisdom,
Son, give me in my need,
    Jesus beneath the shelter of Thy shield.

I lie down to-night,
With the Triune of my strength,
With the Father, with Jesus,
    With the Spirit of might.

HYMN OF THE SUNDAY

On the holy Sunday of thy God
Give thou thine heart to all mankind,
To thy father and thy mother loving,
Beyond any person or thing in the world.

Do not covet large or small,
Do not despise weakling or poor,
Semblance of evil allow not near thee,
Never give nor earn thou shame.

The ten commands God gave thee,
Understand them early and prove,
Believe direct in the King of the elements,
Put behind thee ikon-worship.

Be faithful to thine over-lord,
Be true to thy king in every need,
Be true to thine own self besides,
True to thy High-King above all obstacles.

Do not thou malign any man,
Lest thou thyself maligned shouldst be,
And shouldst thou travel ocean and earth,
Follow the very step of God's Anointed.

THE POEM OF THE LORD'S DAY

THE poem of the Lord's Day, O bright God,
Truth under the strength of Christ always.

On the Lord's Day Mary was born,
Mother of Christ of golden yellow hair,
On the Lord's Day Christ was born
As an honour to men.

The Lord's Day, the seventh day,
God ordained to take rest,
To keep the life everlasting,
Without taking use of ox or man,
Or of creature as Mary desired,
Without spinning thread of silk or of satin,
Without sewing, without embroidery either,
Without sowing, without harrowing, without reaping,
Without rowing, without games, without fishing,
Without going out to the hunting hill,
Without trimming arrows on the Lord's Day,
Without cleaning byre, without threshing corn,
Without kiln, without mill on the Lord's Day.

Whosoever would keep the Lord's Day,
Even would it be to him and lasting,
From setting of sun on Saturday
Till rising of sun on Monday.

THE BLESSING OF THE NEW YEAR

THIS poem was repeated the first thing on the first day of the year. It was common throughout the Highlands and Islands. The writer has heard versions of it in many places.

GOD, bless to me the new day,
Never vouchsafed to me before;
It is to bless Thine own presence
Thou hast given me this time, O God.

Bless Thou to me mine eye,
May mine eye bless all it sees;
I will bless my neighbour,
May my neighbour bless me.

God, give me a clean heart,
Let me not from sight of Thine eye;
Bless to me my children and my wife,
And bless to me my means and my cattle.

THE BAPTISM BLESSING

IT is known that a form of baptism prevailed among the Celts previous to the introduction of Christianity, as forms of baptism prevail among pagan people today. Whenever possible the Celtic Church Christianized existing ceremonies and days of special observance, grafting the new on the old. Immediately after its birth the nurse or other person present drops three drops of water on the forehead of the child. The first drop is in the name of the Father, representing wisdom; the second drop is in the name of the Son, representing peace; the third drop is in the name of the Spirit, representing purity. The child is then ecclesiastically baptized, generally at the end of eight days. If the child were not given this lay baptism it would need to be carefully guarded lest the fairies spirit it away before ecclesiastical baptism took place, when their power over it ceased. The lay baptism also ensured that in the event of death the child should be buried in consecrated ground.

> THOU Being who inhabitest the heights
> Imprint Thy blessing betimes,
> Remember Thou the child of my body,
> In Name of the Father of peace;
> When the priest of the King
> On him puts the water of meaning,
> Grant him the blessing of the Three
> Who fill the heights.
> The blessing of the Three
> Who fill the heights.

Sprinkle down upon him Thy grace,
Give Thou to him virtue and growth,
Give Thou to him strength and guidance,
Give Thou to him flocks and possessions,
Sense and reason void of guile,
Angel wisdom in his day,
That he may stand without reproach
     In Thy presence.
   He may stand without reproach
     In Thy presence.

THE BELTANE BLESSING

Beltane is the first day of May. On May Day all the fires of the district were extinguished and need-fire produced on the knoll. This fire was divided in two, and people and cattle rushed through for purification and safeguarding during the year. The people obtained fires for their homes from this need-fire.

Bless, O Threefold true and bountiful,
Myself, my spouse, and my children,
My tender children and their beloved mother
    at their head.
On the fragrant plain, on the gay mountain sheiling,
    On the fragrant plain, on the gay mountain
        sheiling.

Everything within my dwelling or in my possession,
All kine and crops, all flocks and corn,
From Hallow Eve to Beltane Eve,
With goodly progress and gentle blessing,
From sea to sea, and every river mouth,
    From wave to wave, and base of waterfall.

Be the Three Persons taking possession of all to me belonging,
Be the sure Trinity protecting me in truth;
Oh! satisfy my soul in the words of Paul,
And shield my loved ones beneath the wing of Thy glory,
    Shield my loved ones beneath the wing of Thy glory.

Bless everything and every one,
Of this little household by my side;
Place the cross of Christ on us with the power of love,
Till we see the land of joy,
　　Till we see the land of joy.

What time the kine shall forsake the stalls,
What time the sheep shall forsake the folds,
What time the goats shall ascend to the mount of mist,
May the tending of the Triune follow them,
　　May the tending of the Triune follow them.

Thou Being who didst create me at the beginning,
Listen and attend me as I bend the knee to Thee,
Morning and evening as is becoming in me,
In Thine own presence, O God of life,
　　In Thine own presence, O God of life.

MAGNUS OF MY LOVE

MAGNUS was descended from Malcolm Canmore, King of the Scots. Earl Magnus and his half-brother Earl Hakon ruled the Northern Isles, and while they were in agreement with one another there was peace and plenty within those isles. But dissensions arose. Magnus was eminently handsome, beneficent, and beloved. Hakon was lacking in these qualities, and he became morose and jealous of his brother.

The two brothers met at the Thingstead in Lent, Hakon being there for offensive, and Magnus for defensive, purposes. Wisdom prevailed, however, and war was averted. To confirm the peace Hakon invited Magnus to meet him in Pasch week in the church of Egilsey, the brothers agreeing to limit their retinue to two warships each. Magnus observed the agreement and came with two ships, but Hakon brought eight, with their full complement of armed men.

His people wished to defend Magnus, but he refused to allow the spilling of blood, or the perilling of souls. Magnus submitted to his brother three proposals. First, that he should go to his relative, the King of the Scots, and never return; second, that he should go to Rome or to Jerusalem and never return; or third, that he would submit to be maimed, gouged, or slain. Hakon spurned all the proposals save the last, and Magnus was put to death on the 14th of April, 1115, to the great grief of his people.

Those who were in peril prayed to Magnus and were rescued, and those who were sick came to his grave and were healed. Pilgrims flocked to his tomb to keep vigil at his shrine, and be cured of their leprosy of body or of soul.

O MAGNUS of my love,
Thou it is who would'st us guide,
Thou fragrant body of grace,
    Remember us.

Remember us, thou Saint of power,
Who didst encompass and protect the people,
Succour thou us in our distress,
　　Nor forsake us.

Lift our flocks to the hills,
Quell the wolf and the fox,
Ward from us spectre, giant, fury,
　　And oppression.

Surround cows and herds,
Surround sheep and lambs;
Keep from them the water-vole,
　　And the field-vole.

Sprinkle dew from the sky upon kine,
Give growth to grass, and corn, and sap to plants,
Water-cress, deer's-grass, 'ceis,' burdock,
　　And daisy.

O Magnus of fame,
On the barque of the heroes,
On the crests of the waves,
On the sea, on the land,
　　Aid and preserve us.

HYMN OF THE BELTANE PROCESSION

On the first day of May the people of the crofter townland are up betimes and busy as bees about to swarm. This is the day of migrating from townland to moorland, from the winter homestead to the summer sheiling (a hut or shelter). The summer of their joy is come, the summer of the sheiling, the song, the pipe, and the dance, when the people ascend the hill overlooking the distant sea from among the fronded ferns and fragrant heather, where neighbour meets neighbour, and lover meets lover. All the families of the townland bring their different flocks together at a particular place and drive the whole away. The sheep lead; the cattle follow according to their ages; then come the goats, and finally the horses, laden with domestic gear of various kinds. The men carry burdens of spades, sticks, pins, ropes, and other things that may be needed to repair their summer huts, while the women carry bedding, meal, and dairy utensils. About their waists the women wear a cord of wool, or a belt of leather underneath which their skirts are drawn up and fastened, to enable them to walk the moor with greater ease. When the people meet, they greet each other with great cordiality, as if they had not seen one another for months or even years, instead of probably only a few days before. There are endless noises in the herd: sheep bleat for their lambs, lambs for their mothers, cows low for their calves, and the calves respond, mares neigh for their foals, and foals whinny in reply to their dams as they lightly skip and scamper, curveting in and out, little dreaming of coming work and hard fare. The men give directions, several at a time; the women knit their stockings and sing their songs, walking free and erect as if there were no burdens on their backs or on their hearts, nor any sin or sorrow in the world so far as they are concerned.

Ranged along on either side of the procession are barefooted, bareheaded comely girls and sturdy boys, and sagacious dogs who every now and then, and every here and there, have a neck-and-neck race with some perverse young beast, unwillingly driven from his home. All who meet them on the way invoke the safe shepherding of the Son of Mary on man and beast.

 VALIANT Michael of the white steeds,
Who subdued the Dragon of blood,
For love of God, for pains of Mary's Son,
Spread thy wing over us, shield us all,
    Spread thy wing over us, shield us all.

Mary beloved! Mother of the White Lamb,
Shield, oh shield us, pure Virgin of nobleness,
And Bride the beauteous, shepherdess of the flocks.
Safeguard thou our cattle, surround us together,
    Safeguard thou our cattle, surround us together.

And Columba, beneficent, benign,
In name of Father, and of Son, and of Spirit Holy,
Through the Three-in-One, through the Trinity,
Encompass thou ourselves, shield our procession,
    Encompass thou ourselves, shield our procession.

Oh Father! O Son! O Spirit Holy!
Be the Triune with us day and night,
On the machair plain or on the mountain ridge
Be the Triune with us and His arm around our head,
    Be the Triune with us and His arm around our head.

BARRA FISHERMEN—
    O Father! O Son! O Spirit Holy!
Be thou, Three-One, with us day and night,
And on the back of the wave as on the mountain side
Our Mother shall be with us with her arm under our head.
    And on the back of the wave as on the mountain side
        Our Mother shall be with us with her arm under
        our head.

MICHAEL, THE VICTORIOUS

St Michael is the Neptune of the Gael. He is the patron saint of the sea, and of maritime lands, of boats and boatmen, of horses and horsemen.

On the 29th of September a festival in honour of St Michael is held throughout the Western Coasts and Isles. This is much the most imposing pageant and much the most popular demonstration of the Celtic year. To the young the Day is a day of promise, to the old a day of fulfilment, to the aged a day of retrospect. It is a day when pagan cult and Christian doctrine meet and mingle like the lights and shadows on their own Highland hills.

Some days before the festival of St Michael the women and girls go to the fields and plains of the townland to procure carrots. The afternoon of the Sunday immediately preceding St Michael's Day is specially devoted to this purpose, and on this account is known as 'Domhnach Curran' —Carrot Sunday. The many brightly-clad figures moving to and fro, in and out, like the figures in a kaleidoscope, are singularly pretty and picturesque. Each woman intones a rune to her own tune and time irrespective of those around her.

The people do not retire to rest on the Eve of St Michael. The women are engaged all night on baking 'struan,' on household matters, and on matters personal to themselves and to others. A cake called 'struan Micheil' is made of all the cereals grown on the farm during the year. It represents the fruits of the field, as the lamb represents the fruits of the flocks. Oats, bere, and rye are the only cereals grown in the Isles. These are fanned on the floor, ground in the quern, and their meal in equal parts used in the struan. The struan should contain a peck of meal, and should to be baked on 'uinicinn,' a lamb-skin. The meal is moistened with sheep's milk, the sheep being deemed the most sacred animal. For this purpose the ewes are retained in milk till St Michael's Eve, after which they are allowed to remain in the hill and to run dry. The struan is baked by the eldest daughter of the family, guided by her mother, and assisted by her eager sisters. This cake is called family struan, large struan, and communal struan. Small struans are made for individual members of the family by mothers, daughters, sisters, and trusted servants. These are known as little struans and by the names of those for whom they are made. If a member of the family be absent or dead, a struan is made in his or her name. This struan is shared among the family and special friends of the absent one in his or her name, or given to the poor who have no corn of their own. In mixing the meal of the individual struan, the woman kneading it mentions the name of the person for whom it is being made. A male lamb, without spot or blemish, is slain. This lamb is called 'Uan Micheil,' the Michael Lamb.

The men are out and in watching their horses in the fields and stables. It is permissible on this night to appropriate a horse, wherever found and by whatever means, on which to make the pilgrimage and to perform the circuiting. The people act upon this ancient privilege and steal horses without compunction, owners and stealers watching and outwitting and circumventing one another. It is obligatory to leave one horse with the owner to carry himself and his wife on the pilgrimage and to make the circuiting, but this may be the worst horse in the townland. No apology is offered or expected for this appropriation provided the horse be returned uninjured; and even if it be injured, no adequate redress is obtained.

On the morning of the Feast of Michael all within reach go to early mass. They take their struans with them to church to be blessed of the priest. At this festal service the priest exhorts the people to praise their guardian angel Michael for his leading and their Father God for His corn and wool, fruits of the field and fruits of the flocks, which He has bestowed on them, while the foodless and the fatherless among them are commended to the fatherhood of God and to the care of His people.

On returning from mass the people take the Michael food and having made the sign of the cross of Christ the father cuts the struan into small sections, retaining in the parts the form of the whole. And he cuts up the lamb into small pieces. He places the board with the bread and the flesh on the centre of the table. Then the family, standing round, and holding a bit of struan in the left hand and a piece of lamb in the right, raise the triumphal song of Michael, in praise of Michael, who guards and guides them, and in praise of God, who gives them food and clothing, health, and blessing withal. The man and his wife put struan into one beehive basket, and lamb into another, and go out to distribute them among the poor of the neighbourhood who have no fruits nor flocks themselves.

After the father and mother have distributed their gifts to the poor, the family mount their horses and set out on their pilgrimage to perform the circuiting of St Michael's burying-ground. None remain at home save the very old and the very young, to whom is assigned for the day the duty of tending the sheep, herding the cattle, and guarding the corn. The people of the different hills, glens, islands, and townlands join the procession on the way, and all travel along together, the crowded cavalcade gaily clad in stuffs and stripes and tartans whose fineness of texture and brilliancy of colouring are charming to see, is impossible to describe. The air is full of salutations and cordialties. Even the whinnying, neighing, restive horses seem to know and to feel that this is the Day of their patron saint the holy archangel.

On reaching their destination the people crowd into and round the simple prayer-house. The doors and windows of the little oratory are open, and the people kneeling without join those kneeling within in earnest supplication that all may go well with them for the day. And commending themselves and their horses to the leading of the valiant, glorious archangel of the cornered shield and flaming sword, the people remount their horses to make the circuiting of the burial ground. The great crowd starts from the east and follows the course of the sun in the name of God, in the name of Christ, in the name of Spirit. The priest leads the way riding on a white horse, his grey hair and white robe waving in the autumn breeze.

Having performed the professional pilgrimage round the graves of their fathers, the people hasten to the 'oda'—the scene of the athletics of the men and the racing of the horses. The games and races excite much interest. The riders in the races ride without bonnet, without shoes, clothed only in a shirt and small trousers. All ride without saddle, some without bridle, guiding and driving their horses with a hard slender tangle in each hand. Some circuiting goes on all day, principally among the old and the young—the old teaching the young the mysteries of the circuiting and the customs of the olden times. Here and there young men and maidens ride about and wander away, converting the sandy knolls and grassy dells of the fragrant 'machair' into Arcadian plains and Eden groves.

On the night of St Michael a ball is held in every townland. The leading piper selects the place for the ball, generally the house of largest size and of evenest floor. Every man present contributes a sixpence, or its equivalent in farm produce, usually in grain, towards paying the piper if he be a married man; if not, he accepts nothing. Several pipers, fiddlers, and players of other instruments relieve one another during the night.

Chiefs and chieftains, tacksmen and tenants, men and women, old and young, rich and poor, mingle in the pilgrimage, in the service, in the circuiting, in the games and races, in the dancing and the merry-making.

The granddame of eighty and the granddaughter of eight, the grandsire of ninety and the grandson of nine, all take much interest in the festival of St Michael. The old and the young who do not go to the ball entertain one another at their homes, exchanging 'struans' and carrots and homely gifts in token of friendship and neighbourliness. The pilgrimage, the service, the circuiting, and the games and races of the 'oda,' once so popular in the Western Isles, are now become obsolete.

THOU Michael the victorious,
I make my circuit under thy shield,
Thou Michael of the white steed,
And of the bright brilliant blades,
Conqueror of the dragon,
Be thou at my back,
Thou ranger of the heavens,
Thou warrior of the King of all,

 O Michael the victorious,
 My pride and my guide,
 O Michael the victorious,
 The glory of mine eye.

I make my circuit
In the fellowship of my saint,
On the machair, on the meadow,
On the cold heathery hill;
Though I should travel ocean
And the hard globe of the world
No harm can e'er befall me
'Neath the shelter of thy shield;

 O Michael the victorious,
 Jewel of my heart,
 O Michael the victorious,
 God's shepherd thou art.

Be the sacred Three of Glory
Aye at peace with me,
With my horses, with my cattle,
With my woolly sheep in flocks.
With the crops growing in the field
Or ripening in the sheaf,
On the machair, on the moor,
In cole, in heap, or stack.

> Every thing on high or low,
> Every furnishing and flock,
> Belong to the holy Triune of glory,
> And to Michael the victorious.

THE BLESSING OF THE 'STRUAN'

 EACH meal beneath my roof,
They will all be mixed together,
In name of God the Son,
    Who gave them growth.

Milk, and eggs, and butter,
The good produce of our own flock,
There shall be no dearth in our land,
    Nor in our dwelling.

In name of Michael of my love,
Who bequeathed to us the power,
With the blessing of the Lamb,
    And of His Mother.

Humble us at thy footstool,
Be thine own sanctuary around us,
Ward from us spectre, sprite, oppression,
    And preserve us.

Consecrate the produce of our land,
Bestow prosperity and peace,
In name of the Father the King,
    And of the three beloved apostles.

Dandelion, smooth garlic,
Foxglove, woad, and butterwort,
The three carle-doddies,
    And marigold.

Gray 'cailpeach' plucked,
The seven-pronged seven times,
The mountain yew, ruddy heath,
　　And madder.

I will put water on them all,
In precious name of the Son of God,
In name of Mary the generous,
　　And of Patrick.

When we shall sit down
To take our food,
I will sprinkle in the name of God
　　On the children.

SOUL PEACE

THE duty of conveying the souls of the good to the abode of bliss is assigned to Michael. When the soul has departed from the body and is being weighed, the archangel of heaven and the archangel of hell preside at the beam. Michael and all the archangels and angels of heaven sing songs of joy when the good in the soul outweighs the bad, while the devil howls as he retreats.

SINCE Thou Christ it was who didst buy the soul—
At the time of yielding the life,
At the time of pouring the sweat,
At the time of offering the clay,
At the time of shedding the blood,
At the time of balancing the beam,
At the time of severing the breath,
At the time of delivering the judgment,
Be its peace upon Thine own ingathering;
Jesus Christ Son of gentle Mary,
Be its peace upon Thine own ingathering,
O Jesus! upon Thine own ingathering.

And may Michael white kindly,
High king of the holy angels,
Take possession of the beloved soul,
And shield it home to the Three of surpassing love,
Oh! to the Three of surpassing love.

THE SOUL LEADING

DEATH blessings vary in words but not in spirit. These death blessings are known by various names, as: Death Blessing, Soul Leading, Soul Peace, and other names familiar to the people.

The soul peace is intoned, not necessarily by a cleric, over the dying, and the man or the woman who says it is called soul-friend. He or she is held in special affection by the friends of the dying person ever after. The soul peace is slowly sung—all present earnestly joining the soul-friend in beseeching the Three Persons of the Godhead and all the saints of heaven to receive the departing soul of earth. During the prayer the soul-friend makes the sign of the cross with the right thumb over the lips of the dying.

BE this soul on Thine arm, O Christ,
Thou King of the City of Heaven.

                              Amen.

Since Thou, O Christ, it was who bought'st this soul,
Be its peace on Thine own keeping.

                              Amen.

And may the strong Michael, high king of the angels,
Be preparing the path before this soul, O God.

                              Amen.

Oh! the strong Michael in peace with thee, soul,
And preparing for thee the way to the kingdom of the Son
    of God.

                              Amen.

THE BATTLE TO COME

JESUS, Thou Son of Mary, I call on Thy name,
And on the name of John the apostle beloved,
And on the names of all the saints in the red domain,
To shield me in the battle to come,
    To shield me in the battle to come.

When the mouth shall be closed,
When the eye shall be shut,
When the breath shall cease to rattle,
When the heart shall cease to throb,
    When the heart shall cease to throb.

When the Judge shall take the throne,
And when the cause is fully pleaded,
O Jesu, Son of Mary, shield Thou my soul,
O Michael fair, acknowledge my departure.
    O Jesu, Son of Mary, shield Thou my soul!
    O Michael fair, receive my departure!

THE DEATH BLESSING

GOD, omit not this woman from Thy covenant,
And the many evils which she in the body committed,
That she cannot this night enumerate.
> The many evils that she in the body committed,
> That she cannot this night enumerate.

Be this soul on Thine own arm, O Christ,
Thou King of the City of Heaven,
And since Thine it was, O Christ, to buy the soul,
At the time of the balancing of the beam,
At the time of the bringing in the judgment,
Be it now on Thine own right hand,
> Oh! on Thine own right hand.

And be the holy Michael, king of angels,
Coming to meet the soul,
And leading it home
To the heaven of the Son of God.
> The Holy Michael, high king of angels,
> Coming to meet the soul,
> And leading it home
> To the heaven of the Son of God.

TO WHOM SHALL I OFFER OBLATION

To whom shall I offer oblation
In name of Michael on high?
I will give tithe of my means
To the forsaken illustrious One.

Because of all that I have seen,
Of His peace and of His mercy,
Lift Thou my soul to Thee, O Son of God,
Nor leave me ever.

Remember me in the mountain,
Under Thy wing shield Thou me;
Rock of truth, do not forsake me,
My wish it were ever to be near Thee.

Give to me the wedding garment,
Be angels conversing with me in every need,
Be the holy apostles protecting me,
The fair Mary and Thou, Jesu of grace,
    The fair Mary and Thou, Jesu of grace.

PRAYER FOR PROTECTION

As Thou art the Shepherd over the flock
Tend Thou us to the cot and the fold,
Sain us beneath Thine own glorious mantle;
    Thou Shield of protection, guard us for ever.

Be Thou a hard triumphant glave
To shield us securely from wicked hell,
From the fiends and from the stieve snell gullies,
    And from the lurid smoke of the abyss.

Be my soul in the trustance of the High King,
Be Michael the powerful meeting my soul.

A RESTING PRAYER

GOD shield the house, the fire, the kine,
Every one who dwells herein to-night.
Shield myself and my beloved group,
Preserve us from violence and from harm;
Preserve us from foes this night,
For the sake of the Son of the Mary Mother,
In this place, and in every place wherein they dwell to-night,
On this night and on every night,
This night and every night.

SMOORING THE FIRE

PEAT is the fuel of the Highlands and Islands. Where wood is not obtainable the fire is kept in during the night. The process by which this is accomplished is called in Scottish, smooring, and in English, smothering, or more correctly, subduing. The ceremony of smooring the fire is artistic and symbolic, and is performed with loving care. The embers are evenly spread on the hearth—which is generally in the middle of the floor—and formed into a circle. This circle is then divided into three equal sections, a small boss being left in the middle. A peat is laid between each section, each peat touching the boss, which forms a common centre. The first peat is laid down in name of the God of Life, the second in name of the God of Peace, the third in name of the God of Grace. The circle is then covered over with ashes sufficient to subdue but not to extinguish the fire, in name of the Three of Light. The heap slightly raised in the centre is called the Hearth of the Three. When the smooring operation is complete the woman closes her eyes, stretches her hand, and softly intones one of the many formulae current for these occasions.

I WILL build the hearth,
As Mary would build it.
The encompassment of Bride and of Mary,
Guarding the hearth, guarding the floor,
Guarding the household all.

Who are they on the lawn without?
Michael the sun-radiant of my trust.
Who are they on the middle of the floor?
John and Peter and Paul.
Who are they by the front of my bed?
Sun-bright Mary and her Son.

The mouth of God ordained,
The angel of God proclaimed,
An angel white in charge of the hearth
Till white day shall come to the embers.
An angel white in charge of the hearth
Till white day shall come to the embers.

SLEEPING PRAYER

I AM placing my soul and my body
On Thy sanctuary this night, O God,
On Thy sanctuary, O Jesus Christ,
On Thy sanctuary, O Spirit of perfect truth,
   The Three who would defend my cause,
   Nor turn Their backs upon me.

Thou, Father, who art kind and just,
Thou, Son, who didst overcome death,
Thou, Holy Spirit of power,
Be keeping me this night from harm;
   The Three who would justify me
   Keeping me this night and always.

THE GUARDIAN ANGEL

A CORACLE was in common use among the Celts. It is a small boat made of
hides stretched over a wood frame.

THOU angel of God who has charge of me
From the dear Father of mercifulness,
The shepherding kind of the fold of the saints
To make round about me this night;

Drive from me every temptation and danger,
Surround me on the sea of unrighteousness,
And in the narrows, crooks, and straits,
Keep thou my coracle, keep it always.

Be thou a bright flame before me,
Be thou a guiding star above me,
Be thou a smooth path below me,
And be a kindly shepherd behind me,
To-day, to-night, and for ever.

I am tired and I a stranger,
Lead thou me to the land of angels;
For me it is time to go home
To the court of Christ, to the peace of heaven.

THE SLEEP PRAYER

I AM now going into the sleep,
Be it that I in health shall waken;
If death be to me in the death-sleep,
Be it that on Thine own arm,
O God of Grace, I in peace shall waken;
　　Be it on Thine own beloved arm,
　　O God of Grace, that I in peace shall waken.

Be my soul on Thy right hand, O God,
Thou King of the heaven of heavens;
Thou it was who bought'st me with Thy blood,
Thou it was who gavest Thy life for me,
　　Encompass Thou me this night, O God,
　　That no harm, no evil shall me befall.

Whilst the body is dwelling in the sleep,
The soul is soaring in the shadow of heaven,
Be the red-white Michael meeting the soul,
Early and late, night and day,
　　Early and late, night and day.

　　　　　　　　　　　　　　　　Amen.

SLEEP PRAYER

O Jesu without sin,
King of the poor,
Who wert sorely subdued
Under ban of the wicked,
Shield Thou me this night
From Judas.

My soul on Thine own arm, O Christ,
Thou the King of the City of Heaven,
Thou it was who bought'st my soul, O Jesu,
    Thou it was who didst sacrifice Thy life for me.

Protect Thou me because of my sorrow,
For the sake of Thy passion, Thy wounds, and Thine own
    blood,
And take me in safety to-night
    Near to the City of God.

SLEEP BLESSING

THE night prayers of the people are numerous. It is touching and instructive to hear these simple old men and women in their lowly homes addressing, as they say themselves: the great God of life, the Father of all living. They press upon Him their needs and their desires fully and familiarly, but with all the awe and deference due to the Great Chief whom they wish to approach and to attract, and whose forgiveness and aid they would secure. And all this in language so homely yet so eloquent, so simple yet so dignified, that the impressiveness could not be greater in proudest fane.

Be Thy right hand, O God, under my head,
Be Thy light, O Spirit, over me shining.
And be the cross of the nine angels over me down,
From the crown of my head to the soles of my feet,
    From the crown of my head to the soles of my feet.

O Jesu without offence, crucified cruelly,
Under ban of the wicked Thou wert scourged,
The many evils done of me in the body!
That I cannot this night enumerate,
    That I cannot this night enumerate.

O Thou King of the blood of truth,
Cast me not from Thy covenant,
Exact not from me for my transgressions,
Nor omit me in Thy numbering,
     Nor omit me in Thy numbering.

Be the cross of Mary and of Michael over me in peace,
Be my soul dwelling in truth, be my heart free of guile,
Be my soul in peace with thee, Brightness of the mountains.
Valiant Michael, meet thou my soul.
     Morn and eve, day and night. May it be so.

I LIE IN MY BED

I LIE in my bed
As I would lie in the grave,
Thine arm beneath my neck,
    Thou Son of Mary victorious.

Angels shall watch me
And I lying in slumber,
And angels shall guard me
    In the sleep of the grave.

Uriel shall be at my feet,
Ariel shall be at my back,
Gabriel shall be at my head,
    And Raphael shall be at my side.

Michael shall be with my soul,
The strong shield of my love!
And the Physician Son of Mary
Shall put the salve to mine eye,
    The Physician Son of Mary
    Shall put the salve to mine eye!

THE LIGHTENER OF THE STARS

BEHOLD the Lightener of the stars
On the crests of the clouds,
And the choralists of the sky
　　Lauding Him.

Coming down with acclaim
From the Father above,
Harp and lyre of song
　　Sounding to Him.

Christ, Thou refuge of my love,
Why should not I raise Thy fame!
Angels and saints melodious
　　Singing to Thee.

Thou Son of the Mary of graces,
Of exceeding white purity of beauty,
Joy were it to me to be in the fields
　　Of Thy riches.

O Christ my beloved,
O Christ of the Holy Blood,
By day and by night
　　I praise Thee.

OTHER VINEYARD TITLES

TWO PLAYS ABOUT GOD AND MAN by Dorothy L. Sayers with new plans for amateur production. (*The Devil to Pay*—A Faustian Drama, and *He that Should Come*—A Nativity Play in one Act.) Best known for her detective stories, Miss Sayers also wrote both theology and drama. Her plays combine the nimble wit shown in the Lord Peter Wimsey series with a real love of theatre and a deep understanding of spiritual truths. $6.95 in paper.

A BOOK OF HOURS by Elizabeth Yates with art by Carol Aymar Armstrong. Like and unlike Medieval Books of Hours, Yates' A BOOK OF HOURS embraces the ordinariness of everyday life and finds it holy. Daily activities and each passing hour serve as reminders to turn to God. Miss Yates is a Quaker whose book shares a serene faith. Carol Armstrong's delicate leaf prints decorate each page in soft red or slate blue. $2.95 in paper. $5.95 in cloth.

DOORWAY TO MEDITATION by Avery Brooke. Both practical and beautiful, DOORWAY TO MEDITATION is in the Judaeo-Christian tradition, yet congenial to all religions. Explained with great clarity, each page is hand-lettered or illustrated by the noted French artist, Robert Pinart. $4.95 in paper.

HOW TO MEDITATE WITHOUT LEAVING THE WORLD. Sequel to the above, this is a step by step, fully explained description of how to learn and teach meditation in the Judaeo-Christian tradition. $3.95 in paper.

ROOTS OF SPRING: A Narrative Anthology. Edited by Avery Brooke with drawings by Robert Pinart. The story is of mankind and the world. The words come from fascinatingly diverse sources, yet seem to speak in one voice which faces reality with hope, love and courageous determination. This is a book of great beauty. $4.95 in paper.

COOKING WITH CONSCIENCE by Alice Benjamin and Harriett Corrigan. Fifty-two simple, healthful meals based on vegetable protein, milk, and eggs. A book for people concerned about world hunger. $2.00 in paper.

Vineyard Books may be obtained from your bookstore or send check to Vineyard Books, Inc., Box 3315, Noroton, Conn. 06820. Add 50¢ postage and handling for each book.